Social and Economic Empowerment of Women

Social and Economic Empowerment of Women:

An Entrepreneurial Approach

Dr. Nisha Pandey

GYAN

Published, 2021

Published by

Gyan Publishing House
5, Ansari Road
Daryaganj, New Delhi-110002
Phone: 011-47034999, 9811692060
www.gyanbooks.com
E-mail: books@gyanbooks.com

Printed at: Gyan Press, Delhi.

Cataloging in Publication Data—DK

Courtesy: D.K. Agencies (P) Ltd. <docinfo@dkagencies.com>

Pandey, Nisha, 1973- **author.**

Social and economic empowerment of women : an entrepreneurial approach / Dr. Nisha Pandey.

pages cm

Includes bibliographical references.

ISBN 9788121220156 (HB)

1. Businesswomen—India. 2. Women in economic development—India. 3. Social Entrepreneurship—India. 4. Women—Government policy—India. I. Title.

LCC HD6189.P36 2021 | DDC 338.040954 23

Contents

Foreword

The Indian culture has a great tradition for empowerment of women in the society. Unfortunately, that is missing in the present era of materialistic world. The more we deviate from our cultural roots more problems are created and gender bias appeared in the society in a pathetic way. Few examples could be cited here from Shri Ramcharitmanas. Conceding the request from GOD's Lord Vishnu accepted to appear on the earth along with the primordial energy (Maya) saying that 'आदिशक्ति *जेहि जग उपजायाण सोउ अवतरिहि मोर यह माया।*'

Means the primordial energy 'Sita' who created the world (bu continuous reactions of electrons called Maya-Sita) will also reincarnate. It clearly shows that only women have power of creation. In another example of Manas, Tulsidas Ji state's that the same power is the mine of all attributes and thus Laxmi, Uma, Bramhani the power of wealth, the power of transformation and power of creation; respectively is created by the same power. जासु अंस उपजहिं गुनखानी। अगनित लच्छि उमा ब्रह्मानी।।

Here, the fair gender is symbolised by "Maya" means reactions of electrons in want of energy, the only mode of world manifestation. At an another place mother of Lord Rama states that if only your father has ordered for exile you can ignore because mother' authority is bigger than father's. But if mother Kaikeyi and father Dashrath both have asked for Vana then it must be obeyed.

जौं केवल पितु आयसु ताता। तौ जनि जाहु जानि बड़ि माता।।
जौं पितु मातु कहेउ बन जाना। तौ कानन सत अवध समाना।।

Thus, in the modern times society must realise the power of women for the well being of the world and redraft it's perspectives.

Empowerment of women is not limited to economic empowerment, it essentially means improving the social, political and economic status of women. Empowering women yields power, strength and respect, to the whole family, society and nation. It means creating an environment for women, a free atmospheric from all kinds of exploitation and prejudice, so that a better society can be visualised.

The book has covered that how reducing economic dependency of women and their engagement in a productive activity will give them financial autonomy and involving women in power sharing in the political aspects, provide them the capacity to analyse a situation in a political and social context. The process of empowerment affects at a collective level helping the national growth.

The Government of India along with State Governments has been putting several efforts since post-independence period to uplift women status in general. Attempts were made by the Governments to address the issues through employment, empowerment, labour force participation, education, gender equality and entrepreneurship.

The book has covered that the process of empowerment of women is shifting towards promoting women entrepreneurship to motivating women to participate in the economic activities. The book has covered the women who are being benefited through various government schemes implemented in assistance with non-governmental organisations too. It is coming out from the study that the initiatives taken by Central Government, State Governments and NGOs are boosting self-confidence, increasing the purchasing power and decision-making power, leading to women empowerment. The book has covered that how entrepreneurial activities among women can provide them confidence, decision making power and respect in the family. It, therefore, addresses the economical, socio-cultural, inter-personal, psychological, political and legal domains of empowerment. Dr. Pandey, in this book, has analysed all the aspects related to fair gender, gender gaps, gender budgeting, emergences of various committees and plans to promote women in every field of development in five year plans. From analyzing developmental plans and policies in his book, it is clear that the economic empowerment of women is a prerequisite for attaining sustainable development and achieving all the Sustainable Development Goals (SDGs) linked to women in all the aspects of development. Gender equality and empowered women are catalysts for multiplying development efforts. Investments in gender equality yield the highest return of all developmental investments.

Education and training are essential components of woman's empowerment and development. Promoting and providing skill training is a key to improving household productivity, employability and income-earning opportunities for women and promoting environmentally sustainable development and livelihood. Economic empowerment is central to the overall empowerment of women, and financial inclusion is an important part of this.

Book inclusively covered holistic approach of women's empowerment and imparting them meaningful life. This book will certainly cater the need to researchers and prove milestone for them.

I congratulate her for this excellent piece of work.

Prof. S. P. Gautam
Former Vice Chancellor, R.D. University, Jabalpur, M.P.
Chairman- Ganga Pollution Evaluation Committee, New Delhi
Member recruitment and Assessment board (CSIR-RAB), New Delhi
Expert Member E30W, CSIR, NEERI, Nagpur.

Acknowledgement

Empowerment of women essentially means improving the social, political and economic status of women, especially the traditional underprivileged one. It means creating an environment where women are free from any kind of physical, mental abuse, exploitation, and prejudice that they are the most vulnerable section in the society. Although the participation of women in the local democracy has increased over the years, yet it has failed to achieve the desired outcome of empowering them to as much extent so that they are able to make a significant impact in the male dominated society.

The notion of women's empowerment has long been legitimised internationally, what comprises empowerment and how it is measured, is matter of debate in all development literature. This identifies empowerment as being about increasing people's choices and freedom of action to participate. Reducing economic dependency can be a basis for empowerment. Women need to be engaged in a productive activity that gives them some financial autonomy. The political aspect involves the capacity to analyse a situation in a political and social context. It includes the ability to organize and mobilize for social change. The process of empowerment covers not only awareness at the individual level but also the collective level. This results in collective action which again is the precondition for collective change.

The focus of government is progressively shifting towards promoting women entrepreneurship to motivate women to participate in the economic activities. The study examines the perspective of women who are getting benefitted through various government schemes implemented in assistance with non-governmental organisations. The impact observed is in terms of such as - financial assistance, training facilities, infrastructure and its awareness, motivation, confidence, increase in the rate of women opting for entrepreneurship. Studies have shown that such initiatives are boosting self-confidence, increasing the purchasing power and decision-making power, leading to their empowerment. It, therefore, addresses the economic, socio-cultural, inter-personal, psychological, political and legal domains of empowerment.

I am thankful to Indian Council of Social Sciences Research (ICSSR), New Delhi, for giving me support to conduct this study. I am grateful to Ms. Revathy Vishwanath, Assistant Director, RP Division (In charge), ICSSR, for her all time support.

I am indebted to Prof. C.V. Baxi, Ex Director, MDI, Gurgaon for his all-time guidance for carrying out this study. I am thankful to Prof. D. Parthasarthy, Professor, department of Humanities and Social Sciences, IIT, Bombay and Prof. V. Bapat, Prof. at SJMSOM, IIT, Bombay and Dr. Vibhuti Patel, Professor, TISS, Mumbai, Prof. S.P. Gautam, Former Vice Chancellor, R.D. University, Jabalpur, Prof. Phani T, IDC, IIT, Bombay for their input and suggestions.

The encouragement provided by VES Institute of Management was very exceptional. Support provided by Director VESIM, Dr. Satish Modh, Registrar Mr. Arvind Wagmare and Pratiba Wamen need special mention in this book.

I am also grateful to Ms. Radny, Mr. Manish Bahrti and Pranali Jadhav, Ms. Neha Tetali and Ms. Rasika for their contribution in field work, data collection and for completion of this work. I am appreciative and grateful to MAVIM staff and NABARD staff for supporting in providing information without delay.

My family members have given me enough time to complete this work without any disturbance. Thanks Ashish, the constant source of support for my intellectual, emotional and spiritual journey, Manya, for all the affection, care and challenging my assumptions about the world and Vibhu for being unbridled source of joy. I feel proud to think about my parents who offered us their best to prepare us for acquiring and sharing knowledge in the field of my choice.

Last but not the least, I appreciate the efforts of Gyan Publishing House for accepting the script and publishing the book on time.

Nisha Pandey

Preface

Evolving literature on women development is very vast, covering many themes of development. There are enough research studies on different aspects of women empowerment in the context of India and developing economy which serve as a background reference.

Since the third five year plan, there has been a growing focus on decentralised focus of central government, which gives importance to stakeholders who were not the part of previous policy such as SMEs, projects of micro finance, priority sectors beneficiaries and women among others. This focus was reinforced in 1969 when commercial banks were nationalised to shift policy orientation from class banking to mass banking. Further momentum was gained when by mid-70 the role of urban and rural cooperatives was emphasis in decentralised development. By the 1990s, various land mark projects were established for the informal labour market such as SEVA which highlight the role of marginalised women of society, such projects became possible because of increasing involvement of women led NGOs and other civil society. Since the 1990s, various NGOs have taken up causes of women rights in different sphere of society which has further focused on ways and means to improve current level of empowerment. Also, adoption of MDGs in 2000 and SDGs in 2015 significantly changed the direction of Government policy towards inclusive growth.

Empowerment of women essentially means improving the social, political and economic status of women, especially the traditional underprivileged one. It means creating an environment where women are free from any kind of physical, mental abuse, exploitation, and prejudice that they are the most vulnerable section in the society. Although the participation of women in the local democracy has increased over the years, yet it has failed to achieve the desired outcome of empowering them to as much extent so that they are able to make a significant impact in the male dominated society.

The notion of women's empowerment has long been legitimised internationally. What comprises empowerment and how it is measured, is matter of debate in all development literature. Many scholars have conceptualised women empowerment as "the expansion in people's ability to make strategic life choices in a context where this ability was previously denied to them" (Kabeer, 2001).

During the United Nations Decade for Women (1976-1985), there was a conceptual evolution from Women in Development (WID), to Women and Development (WAD) and, finally, to Gender and Development (GAD).

Since the 1990s, women's equality and empowerment have been at the forefront of government initiatives to promote sustainable development. The feminists working in development have played a significant role in globalising the concept of empowerment as a favoured strategy for promoting gender equality and development.

Reducing economic dependency can be a basis for empowerment. Women need to be engaged in a productive activity that gives them some financial autonomy. The political aspect involves the capacity to analyse a situation in a political and social context. It includes the ability to organise and mobilise for social change. The process of empowerment covers not only awareness at the individual level but also the collective level. This results in collective action which again is the precondition for collective change.

Recognising the importance of women in the economic growth of the nation, the Government of India along with State Governments has been taking several efforts since post-independence period to uplift women from their conditions in general. Attempts were made by the government to address the issues through employment, empowerment, labour force participation, education, gender equality and entrepreneurship.

The focus of the government is progressively shifting towards promoting women entrepreneurship to motivate women to participate in the economic activities. The study examines the perspective of women who are getting benefitted through various government schemes implemented in assistance with non-governmental organisations. The impact observed is in terms of such as - financial assistance, training facilities, infrastructure and its awareness, motivation, confidence, increase in the rate of women opting for entrepreneurship. Studies have shown that such initiatives are boosting self-confidence, increasing the purchasing power and decision-making power, leading to their empowerment. It, therefore, addresses the economic, socio-cultural, inter-personal, psychological, political and legal domains of empowerment.

The study also aims to understand the women's perspective on the factors which includes government policy, women-led enterprises in rural and poor areas, competence, higher education, comparison with general enterprise, innovation, leadership, funding, society acceptance, business diversification, global goals for promoting women entrepreneurship, national mission schemes, digital economy, risks, modern business opportunity and barriers. The study has been conducted in three selected village of Maharashtra. Data was collected from various NGO's, women entrepreneurs and women beneficiaries associated with various Self-Help Group's (SHG's) in the Kanave, Shahapur (Dist. Thane) and Vengaon, Karjat (Dist. Raigad) regions. The Mixed method approach has been adopted for analysis of this research. Primary data was collected from personal interviews with well-structured questionnaires and focus group discussions in both the areas.

Women's economic participation and empowerment are fundamental in strengthening women's rights and enabling women to have control over their lives and exert influence in society. Women often face discrimination and persistent gender inequalities, with some women experiencing multiple discrimination and exclusion because of factors such as ethnicity or caste. The economic empowerment of women is a prerequisite for sustainable development, pro-poor growth and the achievement of all the Sustainable Development Goals (SDGs). Gender equality and empowered women are catalysts for multiplying development efforts. Investments in gender equality yield the highest returns of all development investments.

Education and training are essential components of any strategy to improve farm and non-farm productivity and rural incomes. Skill development is a key to improving household productivity, employability and income-earning opportunities for women and also for enhancing food security and promoting environmentally sustainable rural development and livelihood. Economic empowerment is central to the overall empowerment of women, and financial inclusion is an important part of this.

In recent years, government has played a significant role in bringing about this transition. Right from recognising the need to protect the girl child in the womb to protecting career women in their work place, a number of initiatives have been taken. Empowering woman through her journey to motherhood is an important agenda for the government.

Encouraging entrepreneurship under the Pradhan Mantri Mudra Yojana, the government has provided credit to small entrepreneurs without collateral. 75% of these loans have been given to women, with 9.81 crore women entrepreneurs already benefitting from them under the scheme. Over

47 lakh SHGs have been promoted under the National Rural Livelihood Mission (NRLM). Skill development is another key aspect for raising the potential of our female workforce. Half of the certificates awarded under Pradhan Mantri Kaushal Vikas Yojana have been given to women candidates. Over 5 lakh women directors are currently appointed in companies, which is the highest ever number in India. At the village level, women members of panchayats are leading the empowerment of their villages. To reach the yet unreached women across the country, ministry has recently launched the Mahila Shakti Kendra scheme. Under this, 3 lakh student volunteers are fanning out across the country to directly reach women at village level with government schemes and services for their empowerment. The way forward lies in the conviction that we must have women-led development rather than just women's development. Women need a safe and enabling environment which encourages their empowerment.

The study is classified in Seven Chapters. In the first section, a broad discussion on understanding of women empowerment has been written. In section two literature review of the paper has been taken. Section three and four includes various plans and policies women development. Section five covers gender budgeting, gender gap, research objectives and research methods. Section six is about description of women as social entrepreneurs, interviews and case studies. The last section is conclusion and suggestions.

Introduction

While understanding women's access to education and employment it is found that gender gap exists in both the situations. A large gender gap in literacy exists and participation of girls at all stages of education is below 50%. Similarly, less than 50% of women are employed and a significant portion of them are not paid for their work. However, having access to employment does not mean that women have full control over their earnings.

In recent years, the traditional roles of women have undergone some changes due to economic needs and mainstream women's contribution to the overall growth and development of society. Entrepreneurship development and income generating activities are a feasible solution for empowering women. Micro-finance with Self Help Groups (SHGs) plays an effective role for promoting women entrepreneurship and financial empowerment. It is not only an efficient tool to fight against poverty, but also as a means of promoting the empowerment of the most marginalised sections of the population, especially women. Today, empowerment of women and gender equality has been recognised globally as a key element to achieve progress in all areas. Financial Security studies unveil the fact that SHGs are primarily established for women, and in states like Tamil Nadu and Kerala they have been tremendously successful. NABARD launched a pilot project for women on SHGs in collaboration with commercial banks and regional rural banks. RBI also understands the role and importance of SHGs in financing and has extended medium sized loans to women entrepreneurs with the support of NABARD.

The beauty of women entrepreneurs is the motivation that they provide for other women to come up and participate with equal opportunities and maintain their enterprises. Therefore, this type of growth is truly an inclusive growth in India which will lead to financial empowerment of women. Government of India has ensured that all policy initiatives are geared towards enabling equal opportunity for women. The government seeks to bring women to the forefront of India's entrepreneurial ecosystem by providing access to loans, markets and training.

The MSME Development Organisations (MSME-DO), the various State Small Industries Development Corporations (SSIDCs), the nationalised banks and even NGOs are conducting various programmes including Entrepreneurship Development Programmes (EDPs) to cater to the needs of potential women entrepreneurs. SIDBI has been implementing two schemes for women entrepreneurs namely, Mahila Udyam Nidhi and Mahila Vikas Nidhi. A few government efforts at promoting entrepreneurship and innovation are: Start-up India, Stand-up India, Support to Training and Employment Programme for Women (STEP), Trade related Entrepreneurship Assistance and Development (TREAD), Pradhan Mantri Kaushal Vikas Yojana (PMKVY).

Financial inclusion also mitigates the exploitation of vulnerable sections by the money lenders by facilitating easy access to formal credit. Financial inclusion gained momentum in India since 2005-06 when RBI stressed upon the banking practices which hampered financial inclusion of the masses.

1. **Financial Inclusion for Women Empowerment:**

   There has been evidence that more women taking up economic jobs have led to better living standards for their families –in terms of better financial standing, educational attainment of children and more healthcare expenditure. Availability of credit at reasonable rates boosts the entrepreneurship quotient of women. The government and RBI have realised the importance of supply side issues and started policies like MUDRA Yojana and priority sector lending. Pradhan Mantri MUDRA Yojana (PMMY) is launched by the Honourable Prime Minister, Sri Naredra Modi on 15 April 2015 for providing loan assistance upto 10 lakh to non-farm, entrepreneurs and small scale industries. These loans are sanctioned by financial institutions such as NBFC's, commercial banks, RBI, amongst many other institutions. Under this scheme, MUDRA has tailored three products called Shishu, Kishore and Tarun in order to signify the growth and stage of development of the loans as well as the stage of graduation of the lenders and where they stand. (PMMY, 2020). Payment banks and small finance banks are going to be a game changer in the long run. In households, particularly women-headed, formal savings options can smoothen their consumption and reap benefits of saving schemes and instruments.

Insurance sector has gained penetration in India with policies like Suraksha Bima Yojana, Swasthya Bima Yojana and Atal Pension Yojana. Women can become self-dependent and save for their old age without succumbing to whims of children or the husband. It can reduce the gender gap and gives women a strong field to save productively and insure themselves against any contingency. Women especially in the bottom quintile stand to gain from these policies.

In spite of so many efforts undertaken by government and NGOs, the picture at present is not satisfactory. Mere access to education and employment cannot help in the process of empowerment. These are the tools or the enabling factors through which the process gets speeded up. However, achievement towards this goal depends more on attitude. Unless the attitude towards the acceptance of unequal gender role by the society changes, women cannot grab the opportunity provided to them through constitutional provision and law etc.

Entrepreneurship development and income generating activities are a feasible solution for empowering women. In this connection, Micro-finance with Self Help Groups (SHGs) play an effective role for promoting women entrepreneurship and financial empowerment. Micro entrepreneurship are strengthening women empowerment and removing gender inequalities. The SHGs micro-credit mechanism makes the members to get involved in other community development activities. Micro-credit is promoting the small scale business enterprises, and its major aim is to alleviate poverty by income generating activities.

Women's entrepreneurship can make a particularly strong contribution to the economic well being of the family and communities, poverty reduction and woman's empowerment, thus contributing to the Sustainable Development Goals (SDGs). The governments across the world as well as various developmental organisations are actively undertaking promotion of women entrepreneurs through various schemes, incentives and promotional measures.

Availability of credit at reasonable rates boosts the entrepreneurship quotient of women who can start businesses with assistance from Microfinance Institutions or by being associated with Self Help Groups. Availing credit from informal sources especially moneylenders is easier, but is accompanied by exorbitant interest rates, which often turns into a debt trap and ends with women selling their pledged assets, often their valuable jewellery. The government has been taking several initiatives through schemes under various ministries such as

Ministry of Women & Child Development, Ministry of Agriculture and Farmer Welfare, Small Industries Development Bank of India (SIDBI), etc. Following are few of the schemes for empowering women through entrepreneurship.

2. Schemes for Empowering Women through Entrepreneurship

(i) Support to Training and Employment Programme for Women (STEP)

The Ministry has been administering 'Support to Training and Employment Programme for Women (STEP) Scheme' since 1986-87 as a 'Central Sector Scheme.' The STEP Scheme aims to provide skills that give employability to women and to provide competencies and expertise that enable women to become self-employed/entrepreneurs. The Scheme is intended to benefit women who are in the age group of 16 years and above across the country. The grant under the Scheme is given to an institution/ organisation including NGOs directly and not the States/ UTs. The assistance under STEP Scheme is available in any sector for 33 imparting skills related to employability and entrepreneurship, including but not limited to the Agriculture, Horticulture, Food Processing, Handlooms, Tailoring, Stitching, Embroidery, Zari etc, Handicrafts, Computer & IT enable services along with soft skills and skills for the workplace such as spoken English, Gems & Jewellery, Travel & Tourism, Hospitality.

The Government of India recognizes the need for skilled manpower to meet the increasing need for skilled human resources in the country. So GOI has targeted an ambitious plan to train 500 million individuals by 2022 which on an average translates into 42 million in a year. This for calls enhancing and upgrading the existing training infrastructure needs to meet the ever increasing skilled manpower requirements of the country. As has already been explained, NSSO survey 2008-10 revealed that with it labour force participation rate, share of women in recent years has declined. In this context, MWCD through its scheme titled STEP attempts to address some of the skilled manpower issues especially concerning poor women especially in the far-flung areas of the country where women may not be able to venture out beyond immediate surroundings.

(ii) Mahila E-Haat: The Ministry of Women & Child Development launched "Mahila E-Haat" a bilingual portal on 7th March 2016. This is a unique direct online marketing platform leveraging technology for supporting women entrepreneurs/SHGs/ NGOs for showcasing the products/services which are made/manufactured/ undertaken by them. It is an initiative for meeting the aspirations and needs of women. This was done, keeping in mind, that technology is a critical component for business efficiency and to make it available to the majority of Indian women entrepreneurs / SHGs/NGOs.

The National Mission of Women Empowerment (NMWE) under the aegis of ministry of WCD was launched in 2010 with the objective of all-round development of women. The scheme has in-built mechanism to encourage and strengthen the inter-sector convergence and facilitate the process of coordinating all the women related socio-economic development programmes across all ministries and departments. It is the scheme which will act as single window for all women related schemes. To facilitate the scheme in a better way, a national resource centre for women has also been set up which will act as a central repository for dissemination of knowledge, information, researches and data on all gender related aspects and would be recognised as the main body servicing the National and State Mission Authority. The focus areas of NMWE are many but this project aims at three aspects-skill development (through vocational training), availability of finance/access to credit and finally fostering entrepreneurship respectively.

Entrepreneurship constitutes an important part of the economic life of any individual/society and so is the case with women. The scheme of NMWE by GOI recognises entrepreneurship as an important link/contribution that can contribute to women empowerment significantly.

As per the Women and Child Development, E-Haat portal has been visited by 17 lakh visitors and across India, from 24 states women entrepreneurs/SHGs/NGOs have been canvassing over 2000 products/services across 18 categories (categories could be broadened later on). This scheme has benefitted 3.50 lakh direct and indirect beneficiaries and over 26000 SHGs. As recognition of its contribution to women's life, Mahila-E-Haat received SKOCH GOLD Award on 09th Sep, 2016 and also SKOCH Order-of-Merit' Award for the top 100 projects in India for the year 2016.

(iii) Rashtriya Mahila Kosh (RMK) scheme was started by ministry of WCD in 1993 as a national scheme to provide micro-credit to women for their socio-economic empowerment. RMK acts an autonomous body under the ministry of WCD and is registered under the Societies Registration Act 1860. The operational model of RMK involves aid of NGOs or facilitating agencies who are provided with funds which further on-lend to SHGs. RMK intends to provide micro-finance to the poorest section of women and those who are asset less women entrepreneurs through intermediary agencies for income generation purposes at a low interest rate of 6% who in turn can on-lend to SHG beneficiaries at 14% of simple rate of interest. The basic objectives of the RMK are to facilitate access to credit as an instrument or leverage for socioeconomic change and development of women in totality. The RMK further aims at promote the schemes that provide employment opportunities-directly and indirectly, creation of physical as well as financial assets and lastly to create and encourage entrepreneurial activities of women.

The study was conducted with the support of MAVIM (Mahila Arthik Vikas Mahamandal). MAVIM is an organisation working with the support of state government of Maharashtra to promote women empowerment at grass root level. The organisation works for strengthening and promoting the self-help group at the grass root level through training and providing a fund to the underprivileged women. This institutional model was first implemented under the project of Tejaswini Maharashtra Rural Women Empowerment Programme. The programme aims to provide stability and sustainability to the SHG, which helps building in four-tier institution like grass root institution building, microfinance services, and livelihood and women empowerment.

In order to support SHG's, MAVIM has created a well-organised model called Community Managed Resource Centre (CMRC's). This also works in three level to support Self Help Group at village level to solve problems and implement the schemes. Community Managed Resource Centre (CMRC) is managed by the Executive Members (EC) and Representative of Governing body (RGB). RGB is one of the members from the SHG at the cluster level. At CMRC, two experienced sahyoginis are appointed as area coordinator, where one is appointed as capacity building and other is livelihood sahyoginis. The aim of the CMRC is to build a basic level of self-confidence among the self-help group members and help them to train a self-employed entrepreneur. CMRC is working as a catalyst for establishing a service provider institution for the SHG by introducing SHE software for enhancing the quality of the women and has helped in availing micro finance from the private banks like ICICI. CMRCs has proposing repayment schedule and bank repayment amount above 90%.

Today, CMRC is working in 35 villages in Maharashtra. Around 5415 women are part of the CMRC. The function of CMRC is looked at by the Manager who is the in charge of all the activities happening in the CMRC. They have strong records of the accounts which are managed by the accountant who manages the account related to the loans, and credit received by the CMRCs.

From this study, it is clearly observed that women's entrepreneurship can make a strong contribution to the economic well-being of the family and communities, poverty reduction and women's empowerment, thus contributing to the Sustainable Development Goals (SDGs). Thus, governments should take initiative and action at various developmental projects of undertaking promotion of women entrepreneurs to empower them through various schemes, incentives and promotional measures.

Government interventions through schemes such as Mahila E-haat and STEP are creating employment opportunities and enhancing the competency. Yet, there is further scope to improve the existing platform of E-haat by easing the procedure of registration, creation of awareness among women at institutional and consumer level through proper channels of promotion. Also, a personal approach can be adopted by NGO's dealing with E-haat beneficiaries to understand their concerns in making the products available for the market.

In order to raise female economic participation, policymakers should focus on the factors that segregate economic opportunities and lead to low productivity traps for women. Thus, creating sustainable employment models is necessary to avoid such traps. Improving the access to more quantum of funds is necessary as their purchasing power increases after generation of self-employment. Additionally, government regulations could help manage this risk and increase the emphasis on sustainability of the training programmes. The support of livelihoods is increasingly the focus of the policymakers. Considering the needs of the community for the introduction of new livelihoods programme is essential to get the desired outcome for the schemes.

Improvement in infrastructure services and policies reducing transaction costs to markets can influence time-use at home. Measures may also be needed to expand women's legal rights, improve social norms and collective action. It was observed that microcredit is used for consumption and not for productive investment. Access to credit for women for productive purposes can be enhanced by measures enabling collateralisation of loans with cash flow or equipment.

Therefore, it is vitally important that both government and NGOs work to bear all the costs in mind of interventions to make them sustainable otherwise the training programmes and market linkage programmes will be destined to failure.

Chapter - 1

Evolution of Development Dialogue: Women's Issues in Developmental Agenda

1.1 Empowerment and Equality in Development

Gender equality is a fundamental human right and the very foundation for a peaceful and sustainable society. Access to education, decent work, and representation in decision-making processes are not only rights women should have, but they should also get the benefit for humanity at large. In this connection, the UN-supported 17 Sustainable Development Goal (SDG-5) focusing on eliminating all forms of discrimination and violence against women in public and private spheres. This goal also supports reforms to give equal rights to economic resources and access to ownership of the property to women. By investing in women empowerment, progress can be made to achieve SDG-5, which will also help in the reduction in poverty and boost sustainable economic growth (UNDP).

Having a gender-equal society is part and parcel of having an empowered female population. The concept of biological essentialism involves a patriarchal society, accepting the differences between males and females and blaming it on biology (UNFPA). Such thinking strips agency away from women, making it look like nature itself has made women weak and vulnerable. Achieving gender equality, therefore, allows women to become more and more empowered in the real sense. This can be further supplemented with several schemes and government initiatives, coupled with other change-maker organisations, leading to the development of the condition of women. Equality and empowerment, therefore, go hand-in-hand.

Then there is the question of development. What does social development comprise of? Do empowerment and equality lead to complete social development?

The World Bank has suggested that the empowerment of women should be a vital aspect of all social development programmes (Malhotra et al. 2002). In India, government programmes targeting women's empowerment have not achieved expected outcomes of the goals. Women's empowerment can be achieved when women perceive gender empowerment as a meaningful goal worth striving for (Yojana, October-2018).

Since the 1990s, women's empowerment and equality have been at the forefront of government initiatives to secure sustainable development while alleviating the miseries of backwardness, poverty and social exclusion experienced by women in urban and rural environs. In this process, Sharma (2008) argues that feminists working in development have played a significant role in globalising the concept of empowerment as a favoured strategy for promoting gender equality and just development. (UN)

The need for empowering women to participate in economic activities is essential to build a more robust economy. Economic empowerment of women through participation in economic activities has led to women's empowerment in aspects such as socio-economic opportunities, representation in the local and national politics, social equality, legal rights, and community development leading to the national event.

Women's economic participation and empowerment are fundamental to strengthening women's rights and enabling women to have control over their lives and exert influence in society. Women often face discrimination and persistent gender inequalities, with some women experiencing multiple discrimination and exclusion because of factors such as ethnicity or caste. The economic empowerment of women is a prerequisite for sustainable development, pro-poor growth and the achievement of all the Sustainable Development Goals (SDGs). Gender equality and empowered women are catalysts for multiplying development efforts. Investments in gender equality yield the highest returns of all development investments (OECD, 2012).

An inclusive, sustainable economy fosters growth with benefits for all. It does not harm the environment and uses resources judiciously so they will remain for generations to come. In an inclusive economy, decent work means a living wage, workplace safety and protection against discrimination (UN Women Africa). Twenty years ago, 40 percent of women were engaged in wage and salaried employment; today, 48 percent of women are paid wages (UN). Globally, women still work at lower rates than men. Gender stereotypes often define what 'women's work' is, and can channel women into some of the worst jobs (UN Women Africa). Among 143 countries, at least 90 percent have some legal restriction on women's employment (UN Women Africa).

Boserup's model of economic development assumed that it would eventually lead to poverty reduction as economic prosperity trickled down to the poor. The current context, characterised by liberalisation and market-oriented growth, has shown us a more complex picture. After almost twenty years of liberalisation, there is sufficient and growing evidence that these processes have resulted in more significant inequalities in income and assets between and within countries (Cagatay, 2000).

1.2 Feminisation of Labour

The term 'feminisation of labour' is used to refer to the rapid and substantial increase in the proportion of women in paid work over the last two decades (Kanji and Menon,2001). At the global level, about 70 percent in the 20–54 age group are members of the paid workforce. In developing countries as a group, the figure is lower at 60 percent (United Nations, 1999). However, these figures do not capture women's participation in rural and urban informal sectors in developing countries which is usually less visible and therefore under counted.

The trend in the feminisation of labour accompanied by a shift in employment from manufacturing to services in developed countries, from agriculture to manufacturing and assistance in developing countries. Except for Africa, women's employment has grown substantially faster than men's since 1980 (Kanji and Menon, 2001). The difference between male and female participation rates has shrunk considerably in many regions (UNRISD, 2004). Feminisation of labour describes the increased flexibility demanded from both male and female labour, a fallout of the changing nature of employment where variable conditions, once thought to be the hallmark of women's 'secondary' work, have become widespread for both sexes (UNRISD, 2004).

Informal activities, subcontracting, part-time work and home based work have proliferated while rates of unionisation have declined (Standing, 1999; UNRISD, 2004). In the South, in particular, standard labour legislation has applied to fewer workers, because governments either have not enforced it or have abolished it outright, or because existing law is weak and enterprises have been able to circumvent it. However, stronger legislation is not enough. The advocacy of some international organisations for the implementation of labour standards legislation will only help workers if it comes with policies like competition policy, which compel firms in the North to address the impact of their purchasing practices on labour standards elsewhere in the supply chain (Standing, 1999; UNRISD, 2004).

1.3 Development Planning: Principles and Practices

Development is an organised, conscious and continual attempt by society to select the best available alternative to speed up the economic and social process (Waterson, 1965) where it aims to improve the well-being of men and women, especially those who belong to low and disadvantaged positions. It develops strategies which enable schemes for society to avail resources, benefits, and opportunities but also to build their capabilities and potentials (Figure -1.1).

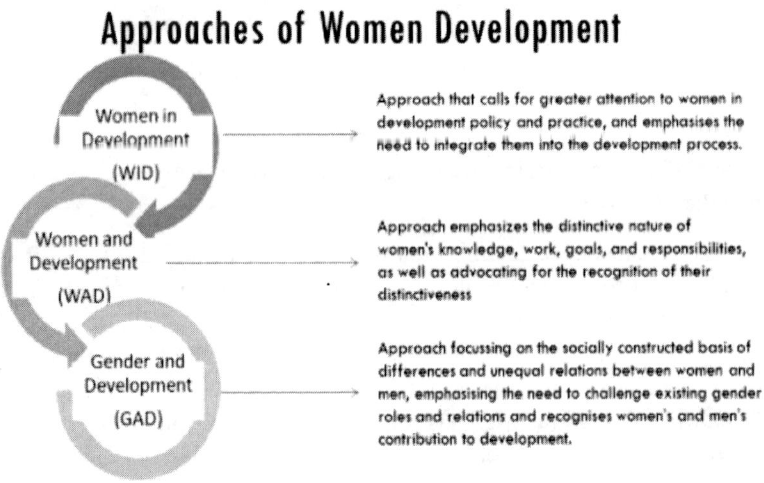

Figure - 1.1

1.3.1 Women in Development

The WID approach was introduced by "American liberal feminists" and focused on egalitarianism, in terms of economic participation and access (Rathgeber, 1990). During the year 1970, there was very little participation from the women the even worse to address the disparity of employment opportunities between men and women in the world. Women were not considered as a part of economic development; any objectives or policy were emphasising on women; this lead women left out from participating in development activities (UNFPA,1994). What is most striking about the WID model is that it did not deal with the disparities and power relations between men and women. Still, it talks about the roots of inequality to address critical issues when discussing women and poverty.

Realising this, it happens to be the essential task of engaging women into development activities, which remains one of the best ways to introduce the integration of women participation into development program and action to improve their position in the society. One of the critical programmes presented for women is an income generation programme with small income productive work. Thus, the best way to attain development while at the same time, women empowerment, is to engage women in the process of development.

1.3.2 Women and Development (WAD)

WAD is a "neo-Marxist feminist approach", and it grew out of the "limitations of modernisation theory" that was foundational in the WID approach (Rathgeber, 1990). As per the Marxist theory, women have always been an essential part of the development system. Women contribute to the economy directly or indirectly explaining that these women work inside and outside the household maintaining the maintenance of society. However, they still sustain in inequality which can be reduced by integrating women into the development process rather than integrating the community into women development.

To improve the condition of women, WAD addresses that instead of improving the international standards of improving the structure and only focusing on improving the condition of the women under the patriarchy, preferably the structure should be formed in addressing the social relations between men and women. This implies that while developing frameworks for women's development, we must attempt to involve women in the development of the structure too and not only attempt to form a just structure without their input.

1.3.3. Gender and Development (GAD)

Gender and development look at improving the current status of development of both men and women equally. It is not involved with the development of any specific gender. Still, it ensures that both genders gain equal access by encouraging political, social and economic conditions by improving the relation dealing with the gender inequality within the society. The GAD approach, developed in the 1980s, stepped away from both WID and WAD and founded in socialist-feminist ideology (Rathgeber, 1990). The focus of GAD was to examine "why women systematically have been assigned to inferior or secondary roles" and also to confront questions of power and agency (Figure - 1.2).

Further, it helps to understand that women should form a union to raise their voice and avail the fundamental rights of food, clothing, and shelter. A Self-Help Group is kind of Union in the sense that there is a collective of women working in the same area, who support each other in times of need.

1.4 Practical Approaches to the Development of Women

The role of women in development is directly related to the goal of comprehensive social and economic development and is fundamental to

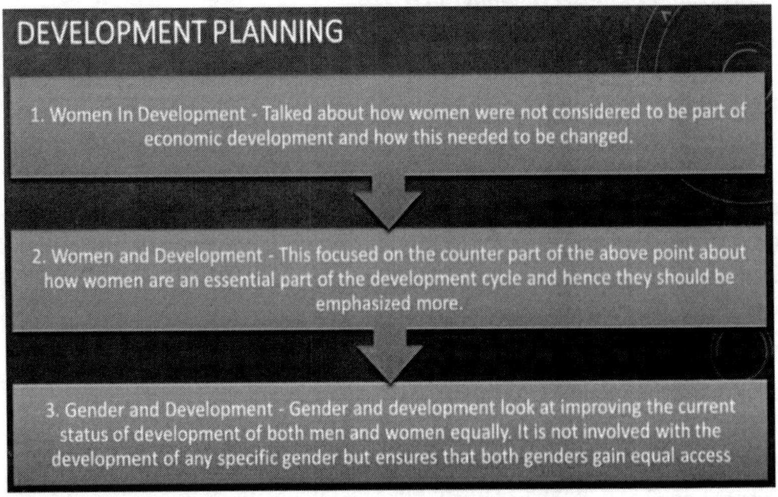

Figure - 1.2

the development of all societies. Development means holistic development, including political, economic, social, cultural and other dimensions of human life like the physical, moral, intellectual and cultural growth of human beings. It should be conducive to providing women, particularly those who are sick or destitute, with the necessary means for increasingly claiming, achieving, enjoying and utilizing equality of opportunity. The increasing successful participation of each woman in societal activities as a legally independent agent will contribute to further recognition in practice of her right to equality. Development also requires a moral dimension to ensure that it is just and responsive to the needs and freedoms of the individual within a social and economic framework. There are various approaches created for better understanding related to women's development.

(i) The Welfare Approach

In the year 1970, the development aspects focused on women's reproductive roles. Mainly the focus was on the mother and child health, child care, nutrition, population control and family planning. This was a significant linkage programme between the population growth and poverty through this focus they wanted to achieve that this economic strategy should trickle down to the poor and that poor women would benefit as the improved position in the economy. (Milan and Rosenfield, 1996).

(ii) The Equity Approach

The equity approach was introduced by the feminists for gender equality, and the main aim was to eliminate discrimination by revaluing of women's contribution and share of benefits from development.

(iii) The Anti-Poverty Approach

This approach focuses on "satisfaction of basic needs and the productivity of women" where income generation and waged employment are the essential tools to help women come out of poverty.

(iv) The Efficiency Approach

Efficiency approach was adopted in the year 1980s, and it is also known as Structural Adjustments programmes of the International Monetary Fund and the World Bank. This approach helps in bringing out the mainstream of development. It promotes women as workers to increase productivity and economic growth with the use of full human resources by providing education and training. This approach understands men's and women's roles and responsibilities as part of the planning of development activities and ensures that women, as well as men can play their part in national development. However, the focus was on what women could do for development, rather than on what development could do for women.

(v) The Empowerment Approach

This approach is closely related to feminist and grassroots organisations. This approach aims to increase the self-reliance of women and to influence change at policy, legislative, societal and economic. To achieve this aims it provides social awareness and increasing women participation in the activity, building organisational skills and self-esteem which an essential role in increasing the empowerment approach (Figure 1.3).

Practical Approaches to the development of women

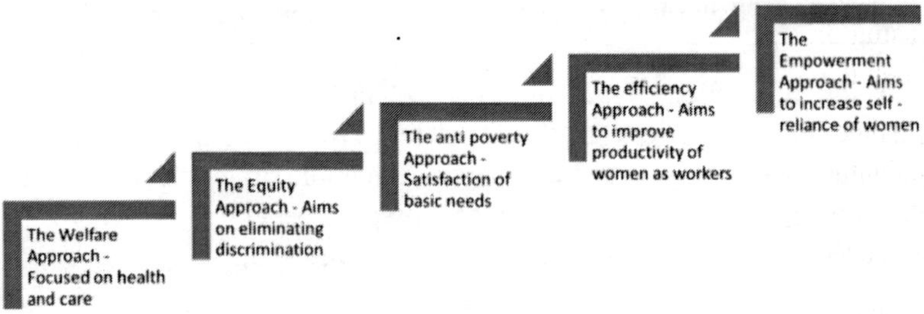

Figure - 1.3

Conclusive Evidence

Empowering women to participate in economic activities is essential to build a stronger economy. Women experiencing multiple discrimination and exclusion. Access to education, decent work, and representation in decision-making processes are not only rights women should have, but they should also get the benefit for humanity at large.

Development processes have led to growth without equitable distribution and prosperity alongside rising gender inequality. The empowerment of women is a vital aspect of all social development programmes as per the World Bank guidelines. Recently, women's empowerment and equality have been at the forefront of government initiatives to secure sustainable

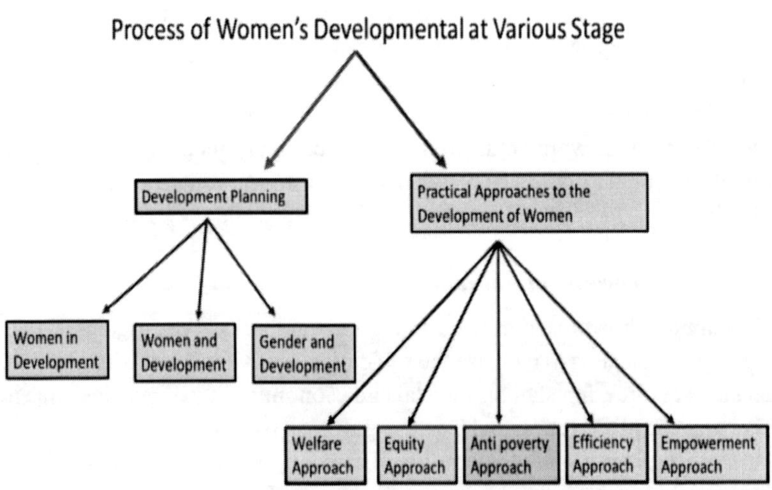

Figure - 1.4 Process of Development at Various Stages.

development while alleviating the miseries of backwardness, poverty and social exclusion. The UN supported 17 Sustainable Development Goal also focusing on eliminating all forms of discrimination and violence against women in public and private spheres in goal number five.

Since, the economic empowerment of women is a prerequisite for sustainable development, pro-poor growth and the achievement of all the Sustainable Women were not considered as a part of economic development and this lead women left out from participating in development activities.

The Women in Development (WID) perspective was proposed and linked with the modernisation paradigm which was dominated in mainstream thinking on international development during the 1960s. But WID model did not deal with the disparities and power relations between men and women. It talks about the roots of inequality to address the critical issues when discussing women and poverty. To improve the condition of women, Women and Development (WAD) addressed improving the international standards of the structure and focusing on improving the condition of the women under the patriarchy. Later, the Gender and Development (GAD) approach, developed in the 1980s, and founded in socialist-feminist ideology with the focus, examine why women systematically have been assigned to inferior and/or secondary roles? And also to confront questions of power and agency.

Development also requires a moral dimension to ensure that it is just and responsive to the needs and rights of the individual within a social and economic framework. There are various approaches created for better understanding related to women's development. Development aims to improve the well-being of men and women, especially those who belong to low and disadvantaged positions. Development policies proposed by various government and world organisations and strategies enable different schemes for society to avail resources, benefits, and opportunities but also to develop their capabilities and potentials.

Chapter - 2

Reflection From Literature

1. Empowerment and its Multifaceted Nature

The notion of women's empowerment has long been legitimised internationally; what comprises empowerment and how it is measured has been debated in development literature for a long time, across the world (Malhotra, 2002). "Empowerment" is identified by the World Bank as "increasing people's choices and freedom of action to participate, negotiate with, influence, control and hold accountable institutions that affect their lives". The idea of empowerment doesn't involve making decisions for the people. Instead, it gives people the freedom to make their own decisions. Drawing from this essence, Kabeer conceptualises women empowerment as "the expansion in people's ability to make strategic life choices in a context where this ability was previously denied to them" (Kabeer, 2001). The primary idea here is an improvement in the previously denied ability of people, which empowers them to make better choices.

Studying Kabeer's concept of empowerment provides an opportunity to link theory with empirical research. For instance, throughout history, women have been confined to play the traditional domestic role in their homes. They were denied economic opportunities. However, in recent years, this idea has changed with more and more women working outside of their traditional roles, mainly due to the economic needs of their families.

With the empowerment of women, more efforts were made to make visible the efforts of women and put the women's contribution to the overall growth and development of the economy. This effort was initiated at the very roots of society; in villages and communities of working women. The growth of Self Help Groups, for example, is one such way to bring forward the contribution of groups of working women. These groups support working women communities, especially those who are poor, to make them more empowered. SHGs are becoming one of the essential means for the empowerment of poor women in almost all developing countries, including India, through entrepreneurship development.

Therefore, empowerment is essentially a bottom-up development which can be drafted as a top-down strategy also (IDEA). This type of empowerment suggests that women cannot be told to empower, but they are responsible for their empowerment (IDS). Careful attention is required to develop the policies for women development because the external bodies tend to position themselves as power over, which helps to position women as only the beneficiaries rather than individuals who are capable of making their own choices. Feminist notions of empowerment deal with these questions of power and agency (Allen, 2016). They behave women as the agents who take the lead rather than mere beneficiaries (UNDP, 2012). To navigate better through the power relations involved in the concept of empowerment, we can refer to Rowlands' classification of power (Rowlands, 1998) (Table 2.1).

Table 2.1: Classification of Power

"Power Over"	Have control over someone. This means power-over can be manipulation, compliance or resistance.
"Power To"	Generative or productive power which creates new possibilities.
"Power With"	The power which makes a feeling among individuals that doing group work is more effective rather than making individual efforts.
"Power from Within"	This concept derives some feeling that there are strength and positivity in each individual. It creates the recognition of one's self-respect, and it helps to accept others as they are.

There are other forms of power described in the literature where a gain of one person is another's loss. This tend to be referred to as power within, the ability to and influence with (Mosedale, 2003).

The power refers to assets such as self-esteem and self-confidence. In a sense all power starts from here – such assets are necessary before anything else can be achieved. A woman who is subjected to violent abuse when she expresses her own opinions may start to withhold her opinions and eventually come to believe she has no opinions of her own. When control becomes internalised in this way, overt use of power over is no longer necessary" (Rowlands 1998). The internalisation of such feelings of worthlessness is a well-recognised feature of women's oppression, and therefore many development interventions seek to bring about changes at this level cite.

The notion of SHG's being the drivers of empowerment reflects Rowlands' "the fellow community power with" other than "power over" choice or "power to" choose.

The theoretical development of the concept of empowerment needs integration of various concept in cognitive, psychological, economic, and political aspects (Stromquist, 1993). The cognitive aspect generally referred as the ability of women to understand the situation of subordination in society at the micro- and macro-level, also to take decisions that are against the cultural and social norms. It involves learning other notions of gender relations and the dismissal of beliefs that form the dominant traditional gender ideologies. This implies that in a sense, empowerment involves both cognitive learning and unlearning. Understanding the concept of empowerment in the mind is the primary step to truly being empowered in reality, for which unlearning regressive attitudes is a prerequisite. This would also involve diagnosing the problem persistent in society that denies them empowerment.

The psychological aspect means that woman plays a significant role in the system and their actions can be meaningful for making others successful. Most of us believe what empowerment is, is a belief that there can be growth and that one can contribute to the betterment of one's life.The fundamentals understanding such as self-respect and the selfesteem elements cannot be taught and an environment and situation can be created where these elements will be developed.

The economic aspect of empowerment involves creating incentives and growth factors that form a conducive atmosphere for strengthening the psychological aspect of empowerment and helping women assert themselves. Minimising economic dependency can be a basis for empowerment; Women need to be involved in various productive and creative activities that gives them some financial autonomy.

The political aspect of empowerment involves the capacity to analyze a situation in a political and social context (*ibid.*). It requires the woman to look at society not just through her own mind, but through the lens of social change. This aspect of empowerment looks at the bigger picture of the society at large. It involves the woman's ability to not just empower herself, but also several women like her. Viewing the problem of disempowerment as a universal one makes the woman aware, which gives her the "ability to organise and mobilise for social change". This results in collective action and collective change.

This multifaceted nature of the empowerment concept must be considered for any kind of mobilisation or change for the empowerment of women. Along with this, it must be remembered that the role of gender in development is incomplete without understanding the socio-cultural contexts. Empowerment involves both an understanding of the self and the need to make choices that may go against cultural and social expectations (Stromquist, 1993). This also involves an understanding of how women perceive themselves, along with a comprehensive picture of the sociocultural context. More often than not, it is this socio-cultural context that influences women's perceptions of themselves, thereby fueling the need for empowerment (Kabeer, 2001).

This socio-cultural dimension of empowerment includes marriage systems and physical mobility of women, which are visible in the broader picture of society. Along with this, socio-cultural dimensions apply to the community and even the household on a micro level. Many researchers have studied that these individual and society level dimensions carry close linkages with each other (Kishor, 2000). This demonstrates how women empowerment is intersectional in nature and thus involves several spheres of life. Therefore, many studies find that all these individual and community level dimensions and their effects are essential in determining empowerment or related outcomes, which is why most researchers who blend theory with empirical work, focus on women's empowerment in their relationships within the household and the local community. This study too, looks at the local community through Self-Help Groups and discusses empowerment of the self through the community.

"Empowerment", decribes various concepts and spread of outcomes and has been used to advocate several policies and intervention strategies more than analyzing them as stated by the United Nations (UNICEF, 1999) and the Association for Women in Development (Tandon, 2016). This can be said because the use of the empowerment concept in advocating for certain strategies has, more often than not, interpreted its meaning slightly differently. For instance, a line of thought in development promotes social inclusion in institutions as the critical pathway to the empowerment of individuals. This has at times, tended to conflate empowerment and participation. Thus, capitalism, top-down approaches to development and poverty itself, are seen as sources of disempowerment that must be challenged by bringing "lower"—the poor and disenfranchised—into the management of community and development processes (Chambers, 1997). However, enfranchisement is merely a component of empowerment, and not the whole sense of it. The crux of the empowerment concept is to give to people what hasn't been theirs before, which helps them make better choices in life. Empowerment cannot only be restricted to a distribution of entitlements.

2. Conceptualising Women's Empowerment

The concept of "empowerment" has often been used in the context of policies and intervention strategies than in the analytical context. This approach to empowerment includes the promotion of social inclusion at an institutional level. For instance, Chambers discusses that capitalism and top-down approaches to development and poverty are significant factors that contribute to the disempowerment of individuals (Chambers, 1997). This idea of bringing about empowerment top-down, has a counterproductive effect. Chambers suggests that this approach must be challenged by the disempowered, by bringing themselves into the mainstream for managing the community and furthering development process (Chambers, 1997). The social exclusion at the micro level arises due to interpersonal gender dynamics at the household level.

Many international development agencies are turning their focus toward assessing gender equality and empowerment (Kabeer, 2001; Bisnath and Elson, 1999), instead of a purely narrow focus on participation or economic empowerment as the only aspect of undoing disempowerment.

'Empowering women' has always been a development agenda since ancient times. Enormous efforts have been done and vast literature on woman empowerment is available, but it becomes difficult to implement this goal. (UN Millennium Project, 2005).

It is assumed that to be empowered, one must have been disempowered. Empowerment cannot be bestowed by a third party. Preferably, those who would become empowered must claim it (Mosedale, 2003). Development agencies cannot empower women – the most they can achieve is to facilitate women empowering themselves. The development agencies may be able to create conditions favourable to empowerment, but they cannot make it happen (UNFPA, 1994). The only people who can make empowerment happen are the disempowered people themselves. With the right atmosphere conducive to empowerment and growth, they can become agents of change for and by themselves.

Definitions of empowerment include a sense of people making decisions on matters which are essential to their lives and being able to carry them out (Selamu and Singhe, 2017). Reflection, analysis, and action are involved in this process, which may happen on an individual or a collective level. Giving priority to the individuals (as opposed to collectives) and empowering them through these development interventions, is fundamental to empowering the society as a whole. However, the power of collectives in empowering must not be ignored, especially in the case of women. This research therefore focuses on this collective empowerment and not just individual empowerment, by studying Self-Help Groups (SHGs) and women collectives.

Social inclusion in the literature is defined as "the removal of institutional barriers and the enhancement of incentives to increase the access of diverse individuals and groups to assets and development opportunities," and it should be noted that both these definitions are operational and they are described as processes and not as end-points (Kumar and Paul, 2017).

"Empowerment for every woman is different and it changes based on various criteria's such as caste, class, position, race, ethnicity". Many development interventions consist of certain challenges. While resources—economic, social, and political—are often critical in ensuring that women are empowered, they are not always sufficient. Without women's individual or collective ability to recognize and utilise resources in their interests, resources cannot bring about empowerment (Sell and Minot, 2018).

2.1 The Process of Empowerment

Kabeer (1999) explained three dimensions of empowerment which are interrelated, namely: resources are explained as pre-conditions; the agency works as processes and achievements are the outcomes. The existence of constraints through customs, beliefs, and norms in society influence women's ability to make a choice (Malhotra *et al,* 2002).

Mosedale believes that a third party can not give empowerment upon a woman if she feels disempowered, but she has to claim for herself (Mosedale, 2005). The external party can only create favourable conditions or an ecosystem which will favour women's empowerment. Empowerment cannot be defined in absolute terms, but it is relative concerning a previous time. It is necessary for an external agency focusing on women empowerment to understand the power relations between the genders in the context, how they are constructed and maintained.

Access to resources and agency in various forms such as control, awareness, voice, and power are the main components of women empowerment (Kishor, 2000). Agency is the essence of empowerment where women make strategic choices and decisions in their life and control the resources. Education and employment used in various researches are enabling factors or sources of empowerment. An additional aspect of this is "achievements" which is the result of empowerment.

Various studies have been carried out on gender issues in various fields such as sociology, anthropology, demography, and economics. Researchers those who have contributed in this multidisciplinary fields have made important contributions to move this field forward are mainly: Kabeer 2001; Acharya and Bennett 1981; A. Sen 1999.

In the social sciences power means power over. As Robert Dahl defined it "A has power over B so much so that he can get to do B something which B might have not otherwise done" (Dahl, 1957).

The second dimension of power is leading the decision-making arena and not letting other people enter the decision-making arena in the first place. The viewpoint that political scientists focus should be "both on who gets what, when and how and who gets left out and how" (Bachrach and Baratz, 1970).

This dimension of power involves the rules and methods of legitimising some voices and leaving behind others (Mosedale, 2003). There is lot of evidence that in inequalities survive by making allied from the deprived. The underdog accepts the legitimacy of the unequal order and becomes an implicit partner (Sen, 1990).

These three elements of power consist of one segment winning against another party through open conflict. This prevents their opponent from being heard which prevents their potential opponent from realising that a conflict of interests exists. These are all the instances of a zero-sum game, for instance by the gain of one person is another person's loss (Mosedale, 2003).

2.2 Empowerment in Development Literature

Oakley identifies five critical uses of the term empowerment in development studies:

(1) Empowerment as participation

(2) Empowerment as democratisation

(3) Empowerment as capacity building

(4) Empowerment through economic improvement

(5) Empowerment and the individual (Oakley, 2001).

Empowerment as democratisation is concerned with macro-level political activity (Lutrell, 2007). Empowerment is seen as the basis on which democratic structures and practices can be built. This approach leads to strategies of support for civil society structures and grassroots organisations.

Capacity-building, is regarded as empowering process. Although there are many approaches, there are some of which require little more than training. Empowerment through economic improvement is an approach which has been extensively used in case of women development and empowerment. Based on the assumption that women's relative powerlessness is principally a function of their poverty. Such interference focus on microfinance and small business development activities, targeted at women.

The United Nations Development Fund for Women (UNIFEM) considers that women's economic empowerment is essential for any strategy of poverty alleviation and defines this as "having access to and control over the means to make a living on a sustainable and long term basis and receiving the material benefits of this access and control".

Empowerment is about power; changing power relations in favour of those who previously exercised little power over their own lives. Batliwala explained power as having two dimensions; control over resources i.e. physical, human, intellectual, financial, and the self, and control over ideology for example beliefs, values, and attitudes (Batliwala, 1993).

It was also discussed as if power means to control then empowerment is the process of gaining this control. An inherent feminist has led some discussion about the meaning of power itself, a questioning of the ethics of power over others (people, Nature). Its substitution by a notion of power as the ability to express oneself. In the latter sense, the concept of power is quite close to the notion of human capability (Cornwall, 2016).

Empowerment is important for both groups and individuals.The poor and powerless in today's world lead fragmented and marginalised lives. Group consensus is a powerful fostering force. It makes people realise the wisdom of the old saying about the bundle of sticks that is much harder to break than the single stick (Lutrell, 2007).

Some of the examples of empowerment from many countries, used group processes effectively and these countries broke isolation and built strength. In other cases, such as the Grameen Bank, group processes have also been used to ensure individual accountability. Individuals tend to be more accountable to groups of their peers with whom they have to continue to live and work.

Keller and Mbwewe describe it as "a process whereby women become able to organize themselves to increase their self-reliance, to assert their independent right to make choices and to control resources which will assist in challenging and eliminating their subordination" (Keller and Mbwewe, 1991).

In some context "women's empowerment," "gender equality" and "gender equity" are different but they relate closely to each other. The research report by World Bank (2001) used the term "gender equality," which it defines equality under the law and equality of opportunity, and the right to have an equal voice (their voice which will help to contribute in the development) (World Bank, 2001).

Women's economic empowerment is critical to achieve gender equality and sustainable development. UNDP provides policy advice, tools, and support for building the capacity of government, the private sector, and civil society to design and implement measures to reduce gender gaps. Women are vital contributors to economies as producers of food, caretakers of children and entrepreneurs and employees in businesses, and as significant contributors to building the resilience of communities to climate change and disaster.

2.3 Decentralising Responsibility and Empowering Women

Gender empowerment goals demand that we listen to women and take what they say seriously. If gender empowerment is to be attained, women's voices need to be heard in a broad range of decision-making forums, from households to national parliaments (UN). There must be space for women to voice their needs individually and collectively without fear. Women's vulnerability to discriminatory social norms resulting from the intersection of multiple identities can inhibit women's active participation in social, economic and political activities. Therefore, programmes that specifically target women and girls should include elements of social learning and practice (Elias *et al.,* 2016). This can be achieved in part by decentralising responsibility and empowering women and their grass-roots organisations like Self-help groups, women collectives, and cooperatives as frontline implementers (Yojana, 2018).

2.4 Status of Women's Economic Empowerment

Economic empowerment is the capacity of women and men to participate in, contribute to and benefit from growth processes. Also, recognize the value of their contributions, respect their dignity, and make it possible to negotiate a fairer distribution of the benefits of growth (OECD, 2019).

The rate of economic participation of women in the labour force has declined over the past decades despite the strong growth witnessed in the economy. It is observed that women's participation in the labour force is more amongst the poor and declines with increase in family income and education, although it is higher among the highest educated. In a study of over 100 countries, female labour force participation was found to be the first to decline with per capita incomes, and rise only when women became more educated and had access to white-collar jobs (Das, 2003).

Among the BRIICS nations, Female Labour Force Participation Rate (FLFPR) is diminishing in China and India, whereas in Brazil, Indonesia, and South Africa, the rate is reviving (ILO, 2013). Most of the decline in the female labour force since 2005 is due to a drop in unpaid female self-employment in agriculture. While female working age population rose by about 99 million, female jobs grew only by 6 million between 2000 and 2012 as employment first rose between 2000-2005 but then declined after that. As a result, the number of working age women outside the labour force grew by over 60 million over the past decade, after accounting for a rise in school attendance (OECD, 2014).

The gap in male-female labour force participation rate amongst emerging markets is highest in India at 50%, followed by Indonesia; the least is in Russia (which is also less than the OECD average). In 2012, the state-wise FLFPR was highest in Sikkim followed by Himachal Pradesh; the least was in Bihar and Daman & Diu (World Bank, 2019).

Rising incomes have reduced the need for marginal labour from poor women, allowing them to stay at home or participate in paid NREG programmes. Real incomes have been increased by the roll-out of the rural employment programme (NREG) since 2006 that provides on average 46 days of work off-season at equal pay (Berg *et al.*, 2014).

According to the NSSO surveys, many women who stayed at home specified that they liked to work regularly either part time or full time, primarily if they could work from home. Access to finance, training, and to have an assured market were factors that would facilitate taking up a job (Sorsa, 2015).

The reasons for declining participation of women in the labour force are several and are complex: the socio-economic and cultural factors are crucial - family status increases if women stay home, housework becomes more attractive than poorly paid market work as husband's incomes have risen, and safety concerns and poor infrastructure keep women from market work (Sorsa, 2015).

3. Self Help Groups and Empowerment

Women's economic empowerment must be dealt with in the right manner, i.e., focussing on not just the participation aspect of women in economic activities, but rather a holistic focus on their empowerment in the true sense. For instance, encouraging entrepreneurship among poor rural women would help them with both financial empowerment and mental growth and happiness; this opportunity of self empowerment would also increase their participation in the labour force. In this connection, microfinance through Self Help Groups (SHG) play an active role in promoting women entrepreneurship and financial empowerment. It is not only a useful tool to fight against poverty, but also as a means of promoting the empowerment of the most marginalised sections of the population, especially women. Thus, women's economic empowerment has direct linkages with poverty alleviation, equality of gender and therefore achieving the Sustainable Development Goals.

Empowerment is classified into three major classifications according to the nature and role of the change agents. (Jagannathan, 1999)

(i) Those that are catalyzed by NGOs.

(ii) The one which develops as moments of people by the change agents.

(iii) The initiatives taken by the joint governments and the NGO's.

All classification has their own merits and demerits. NGO-based experiments are generally innovative, offer flexibility and responsiveness in content and methods (Jagannathan, 1999). With some exceptions, these NGO's tend to start small as well as remain small. They may generate exciting new experiments, but it is very hard for people to replicate or copy these experiments. People's movements too, are fluid in the sense of both their autonomy and the issues they choose to work with.

4. Measuring Women's Empowerment

While transitioning from the discussion of empowerment concepts, authors note that the study on the role of gender in development is incomplete without understanding the socio-cultural contexts where the development takes place. Kabeer elaborates that whenever women assume their subordinate status and perceive themselves of lesser value; their sense of their rights and entitlements gets diminished (Kabeer, 2001). Further, Stromquist adds that women's empowerment includes cognitive and psychological factors which involve an understanding of their conditions of subordination and the causes of such conditions at both micro and macro levels of society (Stromquist, 1993). It also involves understanding the self and the need to make choices that may go against cultural and social expectations. These studies measure the empowerment from a Universalist perspective (Malhotra, 2002).

From multidimensionality approach, Mason points out that the concept of gender inequality is complicated as women and men are unequal in various ways, and this inequality in several settings varies across different dimensions (Mason, 1986). This implies that the occurrence of women empowerment in one dimension may or may also lead to change in another dimension (Malhotra, 2002).

For developing a framework, various dimensions of women empowerment have emerged from several authors. However, the framework suggested by these authors have some commonalities. These dimensions have subdomains, for instance, socio-cultural dimension includes marriage systems, physical mobility of women, etc. Along with this, these dimensions apply to the household on the micro level followed by the community and further the broader arenas. Many researchers have studied that these dimensions carry close linkages (Kishor, 2000a; Jejeebhoy, 2000).

Many researchers point out the level of differentiation in the power relations which also applies to empowerment (Mayoux, 2000; Bisnath and Elson, 1999). The meaning of levels of differentiation may vary according to the underlying subject at the micro or macro level. For instance, in Economics the micro level includes individuals, households, communities and institutions while in sociology and demography the micro level includes anything from individual, community up to polity (Pitt and Khandker, 1998; Rao, 1998). The studies find that both individual and community level effects are essential in determining empowerment or related outcomes.

5. Indicators of Women Empowerment

Charmes and Wieringa (2003) in their article, "Measuring Women's Empowerment: An assessment of the Gender-related Development Index and the Gender Empowerment Measure" attempted to enhance the purview of Gender Development Index (GDI) and the Gender Empowerment Measure (GEM).The authors have proposed gender and power concept and present Women Empowerment Matrix as a tool that links socio-cultural, religious, political, legal, and economic spheres. The authors have shown their concern over the complications in the calculation of GDI and GEM while designing AGDI (Charmes and Wieringa, 2003).

The GDI and GEM are the tools that have been developed in order to calculate the measure gender inequality at a global scale and to increase the efforts towards women empowerment. Authors observe that the concepts like gender, power and women's empowerment have been neglected and thus holistically use those concepts by considering all the concerns faced by the women ranging from physical to the socio-cultural, religious and legal realms, to political and economic issues (Wieringa, 1998).

According to Scott, Gender systems operate in a combination of three vital instances (Scott, 1989). Firstly, gender's physical/appearance differences. Secondly, assigning homogeneity to a particular gender or doing binary division. Lastly, the creation of hierarchy while emphasising one gender's dominance over others which becomes a foundation for power formation. In case of the power perspective for the assessment of GDI, GEM, and AGDI, authors consider three modes of power operation namely oppression, appearance, and its visibility.

Authors suggested Women's Empowerment Matrix (WEM) as a holistic tool to figure out general gender and power issues at a national level (Malhotra, 2002). They established interconnection between physical, sociocultural, religious, political, legal and economic aspects of women. The limitations of this matrix is that it ignores the differences among women and also it is useful only for qualitative purposes where quantitative data might be collected but not quantified.

Though WEM is a holistic process to map out women empowerment in various spheres, the process of women empowerment begins with knowledge and consciousness among women about their oppression and subordination, the presence of alternatives to make critical decisions and the linkage between resources, agency, and achievements (Kabeer, 1999).

Gupta and Yesudian studied the different dimensions of women empowerment by studying 90303 ever-married ladies from every state of India (Gupta, 2006). The authors have used the DHS survey (National Family Health Survey, 1998-99) to develop four indices:

(i) Household autonomy index

(ii) Mobility index

(iii) Attitude towards gender index

(iv) Attitude towards domestic violence

The socio-economic and cultural disparities prevailing in India were discussed in their study using these indices. For all the four dimensions, women's educational level emerged as a significant predictor (Gupta and Yesudian, 2006).

6. Empirical Measurement of Empowerment

(i) Household-Level Studies

The highest number of advances made in the measurement of empowerment has been done at the individual and household level. Researchers have captured the agency component empowerment in a better manner, designing and conducting household surveys which have captured women's household bargaining power, consumption pattern and child well-being (Malhotra *et al,* 2002).

(ii) Aggregate-Level Studies

The progress of Aggregate level studies is still far behind the household/ individual level studies. The studies on the operationalisation of the conceptual framework at the macro level are less developed. The indicators used in these studies capture the difficulty of process and agency as they transit to a higher level. The enabling factors considered are labour force participation, labour laws, literacy, and education, characteristics of marriage and kinship, and political representation by women (Malhotra *et al,* 2002).

Through several studies, it is found that the single or composite indicators like Gender Empowerment Measure (GEM) are insufficient to measure empowerment at aggregate levels (Bardhan & Klasen, 1999; Oxaal & Baden, 1997). Elson (1999) and others have made a persuasive case for why aggregate- level indicators such as women's participation in paid work do not necessarily capture empowerment. Therefore, the authors suggest that instead of using a single indicator or index, a cluster of aggregate level indicators on specific dimension across at least two points in time can be used (Elson, 1999).

(iii) Intermediate-Level Studies

The authors notice the research gap in the empirical studies as it does not address the intermediate level such as a shift in norms, marriage systems, political processes, etc. It, therefore, lacks sufficient literature for programmatic and policy interventions.

The selection of indicators of opportunity structure is complicated because of the existing gap between the method of rules formation and implementation. Thus, a mixed method should be adopted which includes national level tracking of legislation, regulations, and procedures, as well as in-depth probing of how informal institutions operate.

Empowerment indicators must conform to these principles:

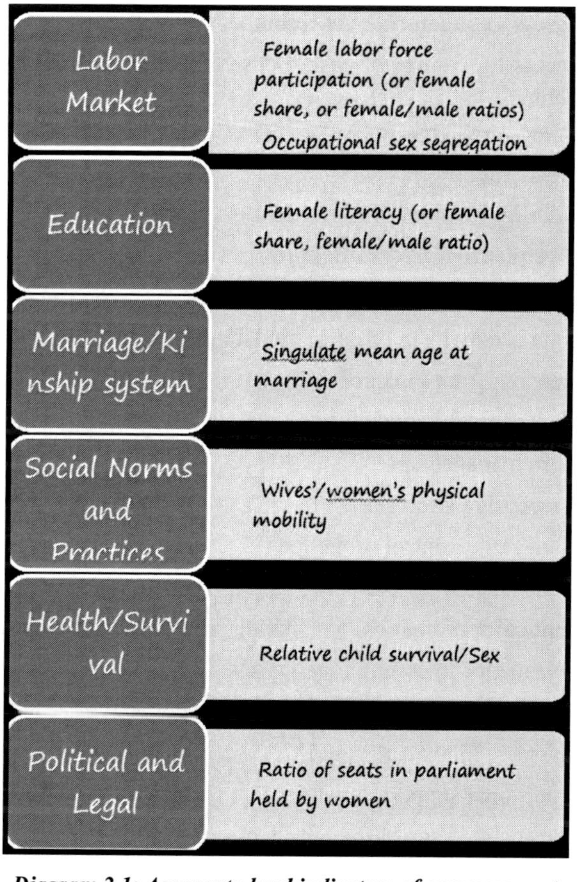

Diagram 2.1: Aggregate-level indicators of empowerment used in empirical studies.

- **Most-Frequently-Used Indicators (GCE Financing)**
- Meaning - The indicators must be able to perform the following: Identify meaningful measurements for a specific dimension of poverty, Permit observation of meaningful changes in both the direction and magnitude of that dimension.
- Causality – It should validate the link between development intervention and expected outcomes (Malhotra *et al*, 2002).
- Domestic decision-making
- Finances, resource allocation, spending, expenditures, Social and domestic matters
- Access to or control over resources
- Access to, control of cash, household income, assets, unearned income
- Welfare receipts, household budget, participation in paid employment
- Mobility/freedom of movement.

(a) Less-Frequently-Used Indicators

- Economic contribution to household
- Time use/division of domestic labour
- Freedom from violence
- Management/knowledge
- Farm management
- Accounting knowledge
- Managerial control of the loan
- Public space
- Political participation (e.g., public protests, political campaigning)
- Confidence in community actions
- Development of social and economic collective
- Marriage/kin/social support
- Traditional support networks
- The social status of the family of origin
- Assets brought to the marriage
- Control over choosing a spouse
- Couple interaction.

7. Mainstreaming Gender in UNICEF: The Women's Empowerment Framework

Sara Longwe developed a Women's Empowerment Framework which has been adopted by UNICEF, which is used to mainstream the gender (IDS). As per this framework, women's development is viewed by five levels of equality and empowerment.

(i) **Welfare:** It takes care of the basic needs of women and does not recognize or solve underlying structural causes. As per the framework, women are just passive beneficiaries of the welfare services.

(ii) **Access:** Women should have equal access to various resources and opportunities to take the education, land and money to make a meaningful progress. A road to empowerment commences when women recognize that they have lack of access to resources which many times acts as a hindrance to their growth and overall wellbeing.

(iii) **Awareness Raising:** The problems of women rise from societal structural and this has to be recognised well. The role of the women should be recognised that they play themselves to reinforce the systems that comes in between their growth.

(iv) **Participation:** Women form an equal participation as with the men. An empowerment happens which leads to an increased participation of women so that they can gain a good representation and they can work together which will help to increase the levels of empowerment.

(v) **Control:** The greatest level of equality and empowerment, where a balance of power exists between men and women and neither one has an upper hand in that. Women play an important role in making decisions regarding their own lives and that of their children.

8. Measuring Women's Empowerment as a Variable in International Development

The Gender and Development Group of the World Bank investigates gender and development issues in an attempt to arrive at a comprehensive and sound policy, to achieve the goal of women's empowerment in its socioeconomic foundation (Malhotra, 2002).

It presents the dual argument for the promotion of women's empowerment as a development goal. It shows that gender equality is both an end goal of social development and human welfare and a means to a more significant economic development by promoting growth and better governance and reducing poverty.

The researchers analyzed a wide range of theoretical, methodological, and empirical literature from the varied fields of economics, sociology, anthropology, and demography in an attempt to understand what knowledge systems we currently employ while evaluating what leads to women's empowerment and examine its relationship with development and reduction of poverty.

"Measuring Women's Empowerment," examines the approaches that have been used until now to measure and track changes in women's empowerment. These approaches are in the loop by the institutional understanding of women's issues and what are the best ways to solve them.

The institutional process that shows developmental policies and provides evidence to show how women's empowerment affects important development outcomes such as health, education, fertility behaviour, income levels, etc. Development of an application framework that can be used across domains to facilitate the desired of the specific aspect of empowerment that is necessary, which will facilitate intensive and specific interventions.

Dimensions Of Women Empowerment Framework

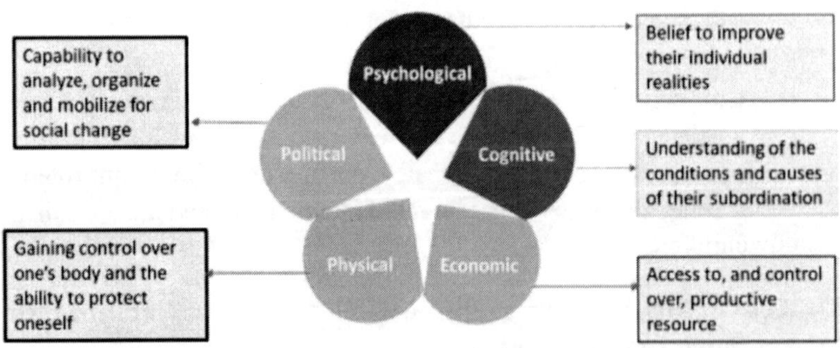

Diagram - 2.2: Resource: Author's creation; Based on Literature Review.

9. Empowerment in Practice: Analysis and Implementation A World Bank Learning Module

The Learning module on empowerment is intended to be a base model that can be adapt to the skill level, interest, context and time constraints (World

Bank, 2007). This module provides a tool for getting an understanding of the concept of empowerment and how it is applied in development practice.

The module offers an outline for conceptualising empowerment that applies the framework to the analysis, design, application, and monitoring of development policies and processes.

10. Framework for Understanding and Measuring Empowerment

When a person or a group of individuals are empowered, they are in a position to make valid choices and can convert their choices into actions and outcomes. Agency refers to the ability of an individual or group of individuals to make valid choices (Malhotra, 2002). Opportunity structure refers to contextual factors that affect the extent to which an actor can transform those choices into effective action. The actual degree of empowerment depends on the extent of the actor's agency and the nature of the opportunity structure.

(i) Significance of empowerment.

(ii) Intrinsic value: The capacity to make valid choices is a fundamental human right and a principle of development.

(iii) Instrumental value: Empowerment correlates positively with growth and poverty alleviation.

There are four types of Empowerment rules

- Allocation rules determine the distribution of goods or services.
- Inclusion rules define who can engage in what.
- Accountability rules determine responsibility and authority.
- Procedural rules determine the sequencing of roles and responsibilities.

For predicting the agency of people, one should identify their endowment of assets, i.e. the resources that allow people to use social, political, and economic opportunities so that they become productive. Assets include things like psychological, informational, organisational, material, social, financial, and human resources that people require in their day to day life.

Opportunity Structure

(iv) Opportunity structures include formal and informal laws, values that govern people's behavior. The existence of these systems affects the way individuals and groups have access to assets and the extent to which they can achieve the desired outcomes using those assets. At times, the formal institutions can contradict or be a barrier in social behaviour; therefore in such cases, it is very crucial to analyze not only formal institutions but also informal institutions.

(v) The interaction between Structure and Agency: Degrees of Empowerment

The empowerment framework classifies three degrees of empowerment for groups and individuals: existence, use, and achievement of choices. It can also be useful in ascertaining degrees of empowerment more directly by evaluating three aspects of choice (Worldbank, 2005).

- Whether an opportunity to make a choice exists (existence of choice)
- Whether a person or group uses the opportunity to choose (use of choice)
- Whether the choice results in the desired outcome (achievement of choice)

11. Where Empowerment Takes Place: Domains and Levels

Along with agency and opportunity structure, it is necessary to study the different context in which the individuals operate.

The empowerment network is classified into three domains:

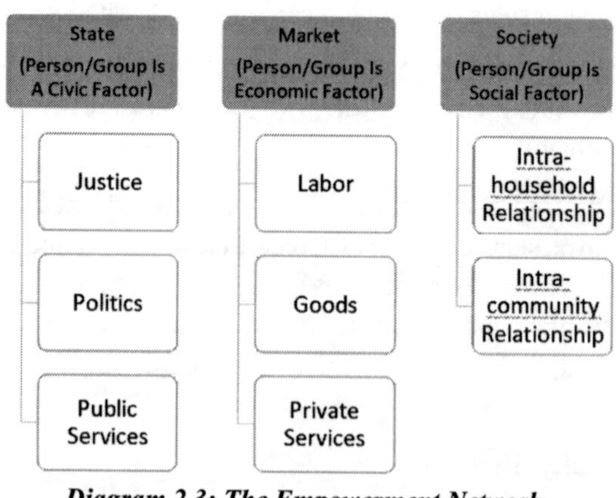

Diagram 2.3: The Empowerment Network.

These domains are further classified into local level being the person's neighbourhood or community, Intermediary level-larger community familiar to the individual but not engaged daily; macro or the super macro level generally refers to the national level.

The selection of indicators of opportunity structure is complicated because of the existing gap between the method of rules formation and implementation. Thus, a mixed method should be adopted which includes national level tracking of legislation, regulations, and procedures, as well as in-depth probing of how informal institutions operate.

Empowerment indicators must conform to these principles (World Bank)

- **Meaning -** The indicators must be able to perform the following: Identify meaningful measurements for a specific dimension of poverty, Permit observation of meaningful changes in both the direction and magnitude of that dimension.
- **Causality -** It should validate the link between development intervention and expected outcomes.
- **Comparability -** It should be comparable across populations within and among countries.

The degrees of empowerment data must be collected from primary sources as the information on it is not currently provided by any other survey instrument.

The framework is complicated and has to be adapted in every context. Similarly, the selection of indicators depends on the purpose in which it is applied.

The issues of empowerment can be embedded in the policy analysis by:

- Identifying areas for inquiry and information or data needed to inform policy formulation.
- Making transparent the assumptions about the predicted empowerment effects of a policy intervention or sequence of interventions.
- Prioritising, sequencing, and structuring empowerment interventions to maximise poverty reduction.

For policy management purposes, empowerment indicators must

- Be consistent and move in the same direction.
- Capture information with sufficient rapidity to illustrate the relationship between policy and outcomes.

- Inform the analysis and design of policy interventions that magnify people's choices in the domains of state, market, and society.

If one has to identify empowerment data effectively, national poverty surveys should be

- Adequately agile to provide "just-in-time" information
- Supplemented by qualitative research that probes emerging policy issues

Major Insights from the Chapter

In this chapter various ideas about empowerment of women has been presented from the view point of researcher point of views and also from the perspective of several developmental agencies.

As per World Bank "Empowerment" is identified as increasing people's choices and freedom of action to participate, negotiate with, influence, control and hold accountable institutions that affect their lives.

The phenomenal work from Kabeer has been identified here who has done path-breaking research in the area of women and development. Over the course of history, women have been confined to play the traditional domestic role at their homes. They were denied to exploit economic opportunities. Although, in recent years, this idea has undergone a change with more and more women working outside working beyond traditional roles, mainly due to the economic needs of their families.

Other scholars have written as empowerment is essentially a bottom-up development which can be drafted as a top-down strategy. As per the research output these ideas suggest that the empowerment for women cannot be told to empower but they are responsible for their own growth and empowerment.

Rowlands' classifies different ways of power expression and how to apply the power equation in different conditions. Through power relation women can realise self-esteem and self-confidence. Empowerment is not one-way process and cannot be experienced with one aspect. Experiencing empowerment needs integration of various concept in cognitive, psychological, economic, and political aspects. Empowerment involves both cognitive learning and unlearning. This would involve diagnosing the problem persistent in society that denies them for empowerment. Empowerment involves creating incentives and growth factors, capacity to analyze a situation in a political and social context because the role of gender in development is incomplete without understanding the sociocultural contexts. Empowerment through economic improvement has been extensively used in case of women development and empowerment. It was assumed that women's relative powerlessness is a function of their poverty. Such interference focuses on microfinance and small business development activities, to give power to women.

Empowerment cannot be bestowed by a third party. Preferably those who would become empowered must claim it. Development agencies cannot empower women – the most they can achieve is to facilitate women empowering themselves. The development agencies may be able to create conditions favourable to empowerment, but they cannot make it happen.

Conclusive Evidence from Literature

It is inferred from the review of literature that many studies do not measure the process of empowerment effectively. Many researchers conclude that enabling factors such as education, employment, real marriage or kinship conditions, or programmatic interventions such as microcredit lead to women having more choice, options, control, or power over their living conditions. In these studies, it is essential to consider the factors that require subjective judgment also.

The process of conceptualising and measuring women empowerment is challenging. Thus, to simplify the process additional iterations need to take place to develop an approach viable for international development agencies.

Chapter - 3

Policies and Programmes for Women Welfare and Development in India: 'Women Welfare' to 'Women Development'

1. Priority Goals for Policy

Gender-mainstreaming and development has been a priority goal in the country's development efforts since the starting of the First Five Year Plan. Gender mainstreaming exercise has been a process of learning and refinement throughout the planning process. The First to Fifth Five Year Plans treated the development of women as a subject of 'welfare'. The Central Social Welfare Board (CSWB) was set up in 1953 to promote welfare-oriented activities for women and children through the involvement of voluntary agencies at the grassroots level. While the welfare approach continued during this period, priority was also given to women's education and maternal and child health services, besides supplementary feeding for children and expectant and nursing mothers. There was a shift of approach from 'women welfare' to 'women development' during the Sixth Plan (1980-85). The Sixth Plan also had special thrust on the three core sectors viz., health, education, and employment. The Seventh Plan (1985-90), continued the developmental approach. The major objective was of raising the economic and social status of women and bringing them into the mainstream of national development and during Sixth Plan 27 'Beneficiary-oriented Schemes' (BOS), having direct benefits to women were identified across various Ministries/Departments at the instance of PMO and were monitored.

Human development was a significant focus of the Eighth Plan (1992-97). It not only encompassed the strategy of enabling women as equal partners and participants in the development process but also ensuring that women were not bypassed from the benefits of various developmental programmes. The Eighth Plan also had special programmes for women to complement the efforts of the general development programmes.

Some major initiatives were undertaken during the Eighth Plan for women included

(i) Setting up of the National Commission for Women (NCW) (1992) to work towards safeguarding the rights and interests of women,

(ii) Setting up of Rashtriya Mahila Kosh (RMK) (1993) to meet the microcredit needs of poor and asset fewer women,

(iii) Adoption of National Nutrition Policy (NNP) (1993) in conformity with the constitutional commitment to ensure the adequate nutritional standard of the people,

(iv) Launching of the Mahila Samridhi Yojana (MSY) (1993) to promote thrift activities amongst women,

(v) Setting up of National Crèche Fund (NCF) (1994) to provide crèche services to the children of working mothers, and

(vi) Launching of Indira Mahila Yojana (IMY) (1995) primarily for awareness generation and economic empowerment through women Self Help Groups.

2. Three-Fold Strategy: The National Policy for Empowerment of Women (2001)

Empowerment of Women as Agents of Social Change and Development continued in the Tenth Plan. Towards this, a Sector-specific 3-Fold Strategy was adopted based on the National Policy for Empowerment of Women (2001). They were as follows (Diagram - 3.1):

- **Social Empowerment** – to create an enabling environment through various affirmative developmental policies and programmes for development of women besides providing them easy and equal access to all the basic minimum services to enable them to realise their full potential.
- **Economic Empowerment** – to ensure the provision of training, employment and income generation activities with both 'forward' and 'backward' linkages with the ultimate objective of making all potential women economically independent and self-reliant; and
- **Gender Justice** – to eliminate all forms of gender discrimination and thus, allow women to enjoy not only de-jure but also the

de-facto rights and fundamental freedom on par with men in all spheres, viz. political, economic, social, civil, cultural, etc.

Three-Fold Strategy: The National Policy for Empowerment of Women

1. **Social Empowerment** - to create an enabling environment through various affirmative developmental policies and programmes for development of women besides providing them easy and equal access to all the basic minimum services to enable them to realize their full potentials
2. **Economic Empowerment** - to ensure the provision of training, employment and income generation activities with both 'forward' and 'backward' linkages with the ultimate objective of making all potential women economically independent and self-reliant.
3. **Gender Justice** - to eliminate all forms of gender discrimination and thus, allow women to enjoy not only de-jure but also the de-facto rights and fundamental freedom on par with men in all spheres, viz. political, economic, social, civil, cultural, etc.

Diagram 3.1: Three-fold Strategy.

3. Gender Action Plan 2016-2021

The WDR 2012 defines gender as the social, behavioural and cultural attributes, expectations, and norms associated with being male or female (WDR 2012). The conceptual framework for analysing gender focuses on three domains of gender equality: endowments, particularly health, education and social protection; economic opportunity, defined as participation in economic activities and access to productive assets; and voice and agency, understood as freedom from violence, and the ability to participate in decision-making and influence political processes and governance mechanisms.

The three pillars are strongly interconnected. Health and education contribute to women's ability to take advantage of economic opportunities and to their capacity to exercise voice and agency. For example, in the post-disaster context, access to social safety nets helps women get back on their feet quicker, their health and education contribute to their ability to participate in economic opportunities and access key productive assets. Gender-based violence is a constraint to women's voice and agency; it can prevent women and girls from accessing shelters during an emergency, and hamper their ability to obtain aid and other resources during recovery and reconstruction.

4. Gender Budgeting

The success of a country in empowering women is highly dependent on the responsive and multifaceted approach to public policy management and implementation, including its macro-economic, financial and trade policies.

The primary driving force for proposing gender budgeting is the need to highlight the marginalisation of women in policies. According to the government, gender budgeting refers to the presentation of budgetary data in a manner so that the gender sensitivities of the budgetary allocations are highlighted. It envisages highlighting the budgetary allocations not only to women-specific programmes but also to quantify pro-women allocations in the composite or gender-neutral programmes under various departments.

Gender budgeting also involves carrying out an impact analysis of government programmes and its budgetary allocations on the overall socio-economic status of women in the country. The ultimate aim of gender analysis of national budgets is to incorporate gender variables into the models on which planning and budgeting are based.

Gender Equality objectives and gender mainstreaming have been in the governments agenda for a very long time however, it happens that a gap exists between the things written in the policy and how in actuality governments raise and spend money. Gender-responsive budgeting helps to bridge this gap and ensures that the money can be raised as well as spent

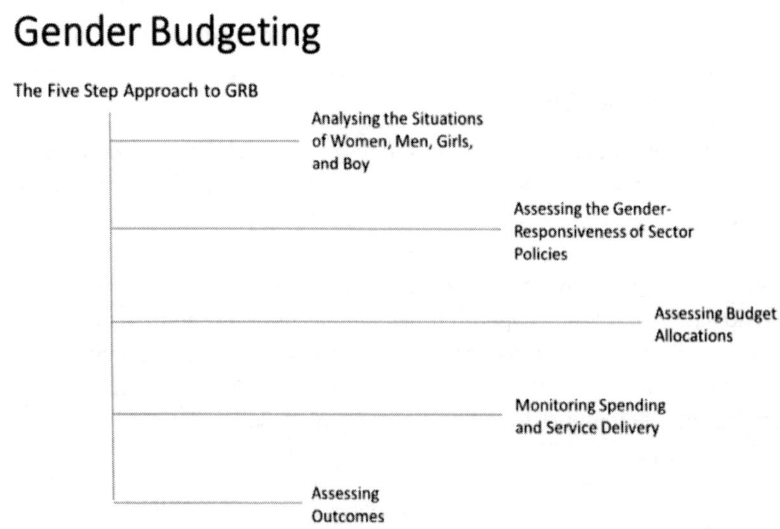

Discourse on Gender Budgeting in India during the last Decade

During the last decade the discussion on Gender Budgeting has revolved around the following issues such as:

- Child Sex Ratio
- Reproduction and Child Health
- Integrated Child Development Scheme (ICDS)
- Social Security for Women in Informal Sector
- Women's Rights Education

in an effective manner. It helped to promote greater accountability for public resources for the people of the country and for women.

5. Gender Audit of Union Budgets

Women's status and women's bargaining power in the economy have a significant role in the budgetary allocations. Yearly analysis of the budget from a feminist angle shows that its today' need to enhance the economic interest of women and their social as well as political standing in the economy. Review of budget from the gender perspective helped to comprehend the nature, character and the part that women played in development. During the year 2001, groups of women and economists focused on gender dissecting union budgets. The Government of India declared the year 2001 as Women Empowerment Year.

A Workshop on 'Engendering National Budgets in the South Asia Region' was held in New Delhi during July 2000 and that was the time when the gender budgeting commenced in India in its true sense. This workshop was jointly organised with UNIFEM and it was graced by many eminent speakers and representatives of the government, agencies of UN, Media, NGOs and Research Institutions, Civil Society and members of the Planning Commission.

Convention on the Elimination of All Forms of Discrimination against Women (1979): Governments' commitments under the Convention on the Elimination of All Forms of Discrimination against Women include removing barriers to women's participation in public life and are linked with the four main dimensions of budgets: revenue, expenditure, macro-economics of the budget, and budget decision-making processes.

6. Gender Responsive Budget Initiative

Gender Budgeting aims to ensure a just and efficient distribution of public funds for the all-round development of the society (Patel,2010). A gender-responsive budget does not focus to create a new budget for women entirely. Its method is to analyze the public policy or raising of money from a perspective of gender, say that the gender perspective involves identifying the implications and impacts for women and girls as compared to men and boys.

A gender analysis of government budgets offers a new tool for ensuring a better match between the government's policy commitments and development outcomes for women recognising underlying gender inequalities and redressing them through the allocation of public resources. Gender Responsive Budgets (GRB) date back to the mid-1980s when Australian federal and state governments implemented them as a gender mainstreaming strategy that incorporated economic as well as social policy and a whole-of-government approach. These initial exercises were called 'women's budgets' because of their focus on the budget's impacts on women and girls. Since the late 1990s the terms 'gender' budgets, 'gender sensitive budgets' and 'gender responsive budgets' have gained wide usage. This terminology partly reflects a move to use gender as a category of analysis. It also represents a pragmatic response to overcome tendencies to misinterpret 'women's budgets' as separate budgets for women. Gender Budgeting is now practiced by many countries with an objective to support government and civil society in examining national, regional and local budgets from a gender perspective and applying the study results for the formulation of gender-responsive budgets. There is no single approach or model of a gender-sensitive budget exercise. In some countries, for example, these exercises are implemented by the government while in other countries individuals and groups outside the government undertake the budgetary analysis.

The requirements of illiterate women living in the tribal areas. However, even in the town, the needs of illiterate women may be very different according to what part of the town they live in, the language they speak, and their mobility within their community.

7. The Five-Step Approach to GRB includes the following steps

Step 1: Analysing the Situations of Women, Men, Girls and Boys

To incorporate gender considerations into the budget, it is first necessary to understand the situation of men, women, girls, and boys in that particular area. While not all men are the same, and not all women are the same, it is vital to have this general understanding before attempting to mainstream considerations regarding each group into the budget.

This step should not only look at each gender as a whole, but should also consider different factors where they may be diverse, such as age, language, ethnicity, socioeconomic status, geography, and disability. Analysis includes looking at gender-disaggregated statistical data, national development plans, government policy documents, official government statistics, or independent research from non-governmental organisations. It could consist of interviews with men and women or household surveys. It could consist of looking at stories and information from news agencies, research institutions, women's organisations, and other civil society organisations.

Step 2: Assessing the Gender-Responsiveness of Sector Policies

The second step is to look at whether the government policies or programmes in a particular sector are likely to affect the gender inequalities that were found in the first step, either positively or negatively. It is essential to look at all policies in this step, not only specific gender-related policies.

For example, when addressing literacy needs, the NPP on Education for All from the Ministry of Education outlines some requirements, policies, and strategies regarding education. Thus, gender analysis of Sarva Shiksha Abhiyan.

Step 3: Assessing Budget Allocations

Once the current situation and gender responsive policies have been identified, the third step was to assess whether the budget allocations are adequate to implement the procedures found in the second step. On the other hand, if the plans are found to be gender-insensitive or could worsen gender inequality, assessing the budget can serve to identify how funds are misallocated in terms of gender equality.

Step 4: Monitoring Spending and Service Delivery

Monitoring is a process to assess whether a programme or policy is being implemented as planned, made progress, and encountered any problems or challenges. Control ensures that activities are performed according to schedule and within the allocated budget and that the impacts correspond to the overall goals and objectives. This step of GRB monitors the implementation of the budget to see whether the allocated money was spent and who benefited from it.

Monitoring should be done continuously throughout the project or programme. Continuous monitoring ensures that if there are any problems or issues, they are identified quickly and addressed.

Step 5: Assessing Outcomes

The final step is to assess the outcomes to find out whether the budget and associated programme have affected improving the situation described in step one. As opposed to monitoring, assessing outcomes looks at the changes that have occurred according to initial plans.

Example: Once the budget for literacy courses has been expended, assessing gender outcomes would entail looking not only at the number of men and women who attended courses but also at the improvement in literacy rates. It would involve assessing whether the literacy rates of men and women had improved and whether there was an improvement in the equity of literacy rates between men and women. It should also look at other factors such as geography, age, ethnicity, etc. to assess whether the budget allocation and implementation of the programme addressed the needs of all groups and addressed the overall situation found in Step 1, and whether the programme helped to reach the goals and objectives of the gender-sensitive policies found in Step 2.

8. Gender Responsive Budgeting in India

In India, after the GR sent by the Ministry of Finance of the Union Government, Gender Budget Cells in various Ministries was set up with the intention of implementation and committing to different Gender Responsive Budgeting (GRB). Initiatives were taken with the objective of influence and effecting a change in the Ministry's policies, programmes in a way that could tackle gender imbalances, promote gender equality and development and ensure that public resources through the Ministry budget are allocated and managed accordingly (Rudra, 2018).

Gender Responsive Budgeting or Gender Budgeting as it is more commonly known is a means of ensuring that public resources are allocated equitably so that the most pressing needs of specific gender groups are satisfied. GRB initiatives do not seek to create separate budgets to address women's gender concerns. Instead, they attempt to view the Government Budget from a gender perspective to assess how it will solve the different needs of women.

With the objective of facilitating the integration of gender analysis into the government budget, this charter for the Gender Budgeting Cells is being drawn up for guidance and implementation by all Ministries/ Departments.

9. Discourse on Gender Budgeting in India

During the last decade the discussion on Gender Budgeting has revolved around the following issues:

(a) **Child Sex Ratio:** The Census of India, 2001 revealed a further decline in the child sex ratio in several parts of India. In urban centres, the deficit of girls has been enhancing due to pre-birth elimination. In spite of demand of women's groups and recommendation of the Eleventh Five Year Plan to revisit the two child norm laws, several state governments continue to victimize the victim, namely poor, Dalit, tribal and Muslim women, and unborn girls. The more budgetary allocation was demanded to implement the Pre-conception and Pre-Natal Diagnostic Test to prevent the sex-selective abortion of female fetuses (Patel, 2010).

(b) **Reproductive and Child Health:** In the National Rural Health Mission (NRHM), the women health workers are not paid even minimum wages and are paid "honorarium." More budgetary allocation is demanded to ensure statutory minimum wages to them (Patel, 2010).

(c) **Integrated Child Development Scheme (ICDS):** Restructuring of ICDS must promote convergence of several schemes of different ministries such as health, rural development, tribal development, JNNURM targeting children (Patel, 2010).

(d) Under the category of 100% allocation for women, institutional support for women survivors of violence need significant attention, but so far not much has been done regarding Scheme for Relief and Rehabilitation of Victims of Sexual Assault promised by the Five Year Plans since 2000 (Patel, 2017).

(e) **Social Security for Women in Informal Sector:** In the labour market, a bizarre scenario is created where girl children are trafficked for sex trade/ domestic work and slave labour in occupationally hazardous condition, sex-ploitation, domestic work/ servitude; young women workers in Special Economic Zone are hired and fired as per the whims of employers and are paid miserable wages. Comprehensive legislation for Protection of Domestic Workers applicable throughout the country is needed urgently. Reasons for non-utilisation of funds under the Maternity

Benefit Scheme must be examined, and concerned offices must be made accountable. In Unorganised Workers' Social Security Act, 2008 (Bill No. LXVII of 2008), particular problems of women unorganised workers must be included (Patel, 2010).

(f) **Women's Rights Education:** The state or professional bodies make no efforts for employers' education about the basic human rights of women workers.

(g) **Utilisation of Financial Allocation for Pro Women Schemes:** UJJAWALA, a comprehensive scheme for prevention of trafficking and rescue, rehabilitation and re-integration and implementation of crèche scheme is far from satisfactory. Three meals per child per day at the crèches recommended by Eleventh Five Year Plan are rarely provided. Except for Tamil Nadu, Cradle Baby Reception Centres for abandoned babies are non-existent in rest of India (Patel, 2010).

(h) **Road and Rail Transport for Women:** India is undergoing U-shape phenomenon so far as women's work participation is concerned. Most of the working women in urban and rural areas travel in overcrowded buses and trains. In the transport sector, top priority needs to be given for women special buses and trains in all cities. For women street vendors, seat-less buses and special luggage compartments in trains need to be provided.

10. Gender Budgeting as an Effective Tool to Empower Women

Gender-responsive budgeting is a tool or means of achieving gender equality and women's empowerment (Patel, 2010).

Gender-Responsive Budgeting Helps in the Critical Functions Like-

- Monitoring of the achievement of the policy goals
- Achieving gender equality
- Advancement towards the realisation of women's rights
- Alleviating poverty more effectively
- Achieving good governance
- Enhancing accountability and transparency
- Improving the allocation of resources to women
- Supporting gender mainstreaming in environment macroeconomic
- Strengthening civil society participation in economic policymaking
- Strengthening the linkages between economic and social policy outcomes.

Looking at budgets through a gender lens shows clearly where the collection and distribution of public money is unequal and inefficient. It also shows how discrimination affects national development.

- Budget analysis and advocacy by citizens brings together technical knowledge for effective and equitable policy-making with political and organising tools for engaging with powerful interests and institutions.
- Gender-responsive citizen budget initiatives compliment anti-corruption strategies. Gender is culturally and socially constructed roles, responsibilities, privileges, relations, and expectations of women and men, boys and girls. In Indian society, discrimination is faced by girls and women through their life cycle.

Gender Budgeting was marked as a "tool" for women's empowerment. The starting point would logically be looking at the constituents of "Women's Empowerment" in various ways like:

Social Empowerment: to create an enabling environment through different affirmative developmental policies and programmes for development of women besides providing them easy and equal access to all the basic minimum services to enable them to realise their full potential.

Economic Empowerment: to ensure the provision of training, employment and income generation activities with both 'forward' and 'backward' linkages with the ultimate objective of making all potential women economically independent and self-reliant.

Gender Justice: to eliminate all forms of gender discrimination and thus, allow women to enjoy not only the de-jure but also the de-facto rights and fundamental freedom on par with men in all spheres, viz. Political, economic, social, civil, cultural, etc. (Vibhuti, 2015).

11. Incorporation of Gender Concerns for inclusive growth under the Results Framework Document (RFD)

Gender budgeting was included in all the strategic important departments including Science & Technology, Department of Biotechnology, Information Technology, Labour, Youth Affairs, Panchayati Raj, Human Resource Development, Health and Family Welfare and Rural Development.

Application of Science & Technology for weaker sections, women and other disadvantaged sections of society is one of the critical functions of the Ministry. Among the key objectives, priority is being accorded to providing support to women for gender parity in Science & Technology.

Under its objective of promotion of specialised human resource for frontier research, the department has accorded priority to the participation of employed/unemployed women scientists. Priority has been accorded to make Common Service Centres sustainable, which includes e-literacy for women as success indicators. Imparting vocational training to women has been accorded priority among the critical objectives of the Ministry of Labour. Under the key objective of 'Engaging Rural Youth in Nation Building Activities,' priority has been accorded to Skills Development Programmes for women. Ministry of Panchayati Raj has incorporated the enhancement of reservation for women in PRIs. The Mission statement of the RFD (Results-Framework Document) of the Ministry of Health and Family Welfare includes bringing down Maternal Mortality Rate.The RFD of the Rural Development Ministry has set gender disaggregated targets for employment generated under MNREGA (Mahatma Gandhi National Rural Employment Guarantee Act).

12. Government Initiatives through Policy, Programmes, and Schemes

The National Commission for Women is a national level statutory body set up in 1990 to work towards safeguarding the rights and interests of women and thus has been working towards gender justice for women in the country.

The principal activities of the Commission include- investigation, examination, and review of all matters relating to safeguards provided to women under the Indian Constitution; review of the implementation of women-specific and women related legislation and to suggest suitable amendments wherever needed; keeping surveillance and facilitating redressal of grievances of women, etc.

The Commission has been in the forefront of the national endeavour to improve the status of women in society and work for their overall empowerment. The essential activities that the Commission has been undertaking besides a review of laws and legislation, inquiries related to violence against women, organising seminars, workshops, public hearing, etc., organising Bal Vivah Virodh Abhiyan, interacting with members of parliament and others regarding pending women related bills, organising Parivarik Mahila Lok Adalats and legal awareness programmes, sponsoring studies on women related issues, etc. A common point raised regarding the Commission is that the Commission has been functioning more as an advisory body. The Planning Commission was established in March 1950 by a Resolution of the Government of India to define the scope of its work

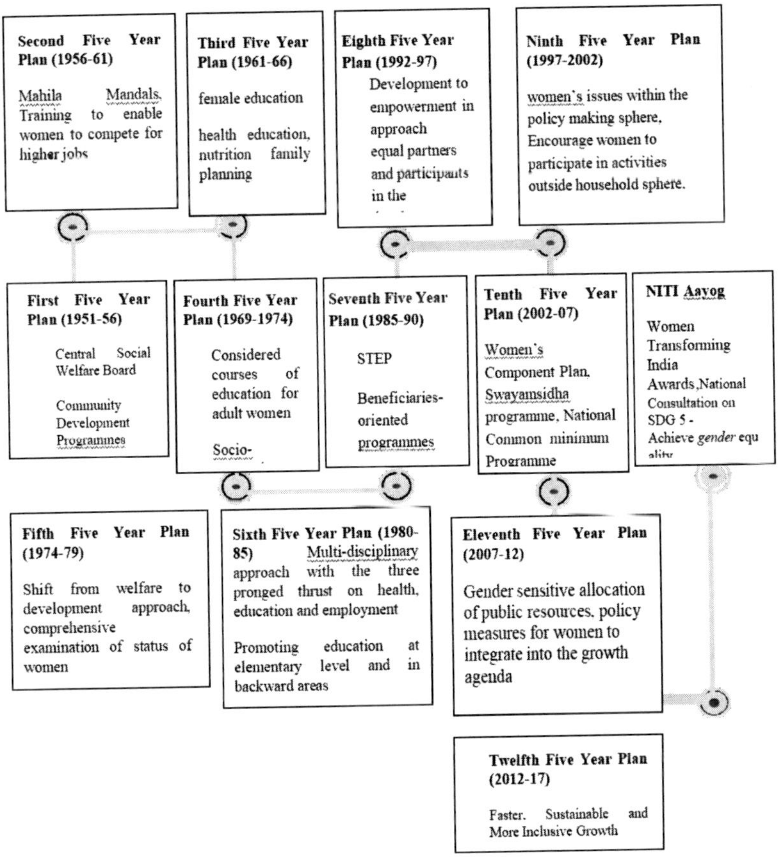

Diagram - 3.2: Source: Author Creation Based on Literature.

into the citizens of India. The Directive Principles of State Policy were established to promote the welfare of the people by effectively securing and protecting through a social order in which justice, social, economic and political aspects.

13. Issues and Policies Related to Women in Various Five Years Plans

13.1 First Five Year Plan (1951-56): Institutional and structural factors in development related to women

The objective of the First Five-Year Plan was to initiate the process of development which will raise the standard of living by giving new opportunities to women in order to have a more vibrant and varied life. The focus on economic planning was to utilise the potential of resources more effectively. In a broader sense, the financial condition of the country is a reflection of the social environment. Therefore, considering this environment is recognised in economic planning.

The primary objective of the plan was to provide equal opportunities for the growth of both men and women by setting up productive mechanisms that will bolster the development process. Along with this, to promote the dynamic cultural progress, there was a need to alter the social settings by improving sanitation, health, and education.

Main Focus Areas

In the given period, the education system was in the transition phase with the scope of experimentation was maximum. There were many organisations which held their examinations and issued certificates to successful candidates. There are various issues that women face in pursuing education such as broader responsibilities at home, suspension of studies. Therefore, to solve this problem, an arrangement was to be made to educate women at their convenience.

13.2 Second Five Year Plan (1956-61): Women Workers

A critical movement began during the first year plan which was women's savings movement which is one such event that could be carried out everywhere. Thus, it was necessary to propagate this movement in a practical and sustained manner.

Education

A significant issue faced while promoting women education was the lack of trained women teachers. Thus, it was urgent need to tackle it by training women teachers and providing them with facilities such as housing facilities for women teachers in villages and some innovative measures to encourage educated married women to enter the part-time teaching profession.

In comparison to men, women face social prejudices and physical limitations. The fact that women have different capabilities doesn't imply that they constitute a lower class of workers.

13.3 Third Five Year Plan (1961-66) Welfare Programmes

The First and Second Five Year Plans have strengthened the foundations of economic and social life which initiated commercial and industrial growth.

The Third Five Year Plan had taken into account the failures and achievements encountered in the development process of previous plans.

Some essential steps undertaken during the first two five year plans were the activities conducted by the Central and State Social Welfare Board in association with 6000 voluntary organisations. Out of which 2900 were engaged in the welfare activities of women. Additionally, 75 urban community centers, 21 production units were established to assist women in supplementing their income. During the First Plan, welfare extension projects were set up, which served 25 villages by providing maternity and child health services, craft classes, social education for women and care of children through balwadis. These projects, along with 134 more established during the Second Plan, have now been made over to Mahila manuals with financial assistance from the Central Social Welfare Board. In the Third Five Year Plan, provision was made for support to Mahila manuals to provide services at about 1700 centers in the welfare extension projects entrusted to them.

13.4 Fourth Five Year Plan (1969-1974)

Women's Welfare

In the Third Plan, 625 condensed courses of education that benefitted 4384 women were conducted by voluntary organisations; 790 holiday camps were run.

During the Third Five Year Plan, Social defense programmes under the Suppression of Immoral Traffic in Women and Girls Act, Probation of Offenders' Act and Childrens Acts were organised. ₹ 2 crores were given as assistance to voluntary organisations for the welfare of destitute children and destitute women. The same was to be continued in the fourth year plan.

The main activities are the provision of integrated services included basic training to women in home craft, mothercraft, health education, nutrition, and child care.

13.5 Fifth Five Year Plan (1974-79): International Women's decade

The Fifth Year Plan happened to be during the International Women's decade and the submission of the Report of the Committee on the Status of Women in India (CSWI) "Towards Equality." The CSWI had comprehensively examined the rights and status of women in the context of changing social and economic conditions and the problems relating to the advancement of women. The CSWI reported that the dynamics of social change and development had adversely affected a large section of women and had created new imbalances and disparities. It was realised that constitutional guarantees of equality would be meaningless and unrealistic, unless women's rights to economic independence is acknowledged and their training in skills as contributors to the family and the national economy, was improved.

13.6 Sixth Five Year Plan (1980-85): Multi-Disciplinary Approach With The Three-Pronged Thrust on Health, Education, and Employment

The Sixth Five-Year Plan (1980-85), marked a landmark in the history of women's development by including a separate chapter and adopting a multi-disciplinary approach with the three-pronged thrust on health, education, and employment. This Plan reviewed the status and situation of women in general and concluded that in spite of legal and constitutional guarantees; women had lagged behind men in all sectors. It stressed that the primary strategy for women's development was three-fold education, employment, and health. For the first time, it clearly spelt out that economic independence would accelerate improvement in the status of women and it was suggested that cells must be set up at the district level for increasing women's participation through self-employment. It also wanted the government to review the adequacy of the implementing machinery of various special legislations passed for the protection of women's rights. It referred, as usual, to the need for increasing enrollment of the girls at the elementary level, thus encouraging the promotion of education for women in backward areas.

The Sixth Five Year Plan stressed the need for economic independence, educational advancement and access to healthcare and family planning, as essential for women's development. So the strategy was threefold, comprising education, employment and health. These are both independent and dependent on the total developmental process.

13.7 Seventh Five Year Plan (1985-90): Generate Awareness Among Women about their Rights and Privileges

The Seventh Five Year Plan sought to generate awareness among women about their rights and privileges. The long term objectives of developmental programmes in the Seventh Plan were to raise women's economic and social status, in order to bring them into the mainstream of national development. It recognised the importance of women in contributing to various socio-economic, political and cultural activities.

The seventh plan emphasised the need to open new avenues of work for women and perceive them as crucial resources for the development of the country. Another salient and critical recognition was the need for the organisation of women workers and unionisation. Under the plan, a new scheme, "Women's Development Corporation" has been taken up for promoting employment generating activities by supporting projects from women's groups and women from weaker sections of society. A women's development planning and monitoring cell was also set up for the collection of data and monitoring of plan programmes. A very significant step therein was to identify and promote beneficiary oriented programmes which extended direct benefits to women.

During the 7th Plan period, the Indian Parliament adopted a National Policy on Education 1986 included a chapter on Education for women's equality.

13.8 Eighth Five Year Plan (1992-97): A Shift from Development to Empowerment in the Approach

The Eighth Five-Year Plan (1992-97), marked a shift from development to empowerment in the approach to women development schemes. It promised to "ensure that the benefits of development from different sectors do not bypass women" and women must be enabled to function as equal partners and participants in the development process.

The strategy in the Eighth Plan was to ensure that the benefits of development from different sectors did not bypass women and special programmes were implemented to complement the general applications. The primary objective of the Eighth Plan was to extend the reach of services to women both qualitatively and quantitatively. Panchayati Raj institutions were involved in the designing and implementation of women's programmes. The approach of the Eighth Plan made a definite shift from development to the empowerment of women. To meet the needs of women and children, there had been a progressive increase in the plan outlays over time.

13.9 Ninth Five Year Plan (1997-2002): Empowerment of Women and People's Participation

An approach paper had been developed by the Planning Commission and accepted by the National Development Council. In this paper, focus was laid on the empowerment of women and people's participation in planning and implementation of strategies. An essential objective of the approach paper was the empowerment of women.

In the planning process, empowerment at the outset means choices for women and opportunities to avail these choices. A supportive environment should be provided to women at all stages by their home, school, religion, government, and workplace. A supportive environment was one that was gender sensitive. In all regional meetings, participants asked for gender sensitisation or training at all levels in the public and private sectors.

The government has set up national resource units for women, which act as apex bodies for promoting and incorporating gender perspectives in politics and programmes of the government. To achieve the goals laid down therein, some initiatives had been launched. They include enactment of legislation to ban sex determination tests to prevent female foeticide. Equally important is the fact that the state governments are also drawing up plans of action to cater to local requirements and ensure the holistic development of the girl child. The 73rd and 74th Constitutional Amendment Acts of 1993 provide reservation of 1/3 of seats for women in all elected offices of local bodies, in rural and urban areas. In the rural areas, women have thus been brought to the center-stage in the nation's efforts to strengthen democratic institutions.

13.10 Tenth Five Year Plan (2002-07): National Policy for Empowerment of Women

The Tenth Plan (2002-2007) has set specific aims at empowering women through translating the recently adopted National Policy for Empowerment of Women (2001) into action and ensuring 'survival' protection and development of children through a rights-based approach, monitorable targets for women. For instance, The Swayamsidha programme, a recast version of the Indira Mahila Yojna, that organizes women into Self-Help Groups (SHGs) for income generation activities. It also facilitates access to services such as literacy, health, non-formal education, water-supply, etc.

One of the basic principles of governance laid down in the United Progressive Alliance Government's National Common Minimum Programme (NCMP) is to empower women politically, educationally, economically and legally. The Women's Component Plan (WCP) involved efforts to ensure that not less than 30 percent of funds/benefits were earmarked for women under the various schemes of the women-related ministries/departments. Women are under-represented in the process of the formulation and implementation of the Plan itself. WCP seems an afterthought, just added on to pre-existing development programmes and projects. The actual experiences of women in empowering themselves need to be first understood and those experiences used as a benchmark.

13.11 Eleventh Five Year Plan (2007-12): Aimed to Raise the Sex Ratio

The Eleventh Plan Approach paper aimed to raise the sex ratio for the age group 0–6 to 935 by 2011–12 and to 950 by 2016 –17. Further, this plan intends to ensure 33 percent of the direct and indirect beneficiaries of all government schemes are women and girl children. It also proposes to ensure that all children enjoy a safe childhood without any compulsion to work.

The Approach Paper to the Eleventh Plan (2007-2012) reads: "An important divide which compels immediate attention relates to gender. Special, focused efforts were made to purge society of this malaise by creating an enabling environment for women to become economically, politically and socially empowered." However, past Plans have expressed similar concerns concerning the gender divide. The strategy for women is confined to three areas- violence against women, economic empowerment and women's health. A major challenge before the 11th Plan was to enable the creation of an environment for women that is safe and free from violence. Regular campaigns of issues such as female foeticide, physical abuse, trafficking, gender discrimination, and domestic violence were organised. Finally, the 11th Plan recognised that a nation could not be healthy unless its women are healthy. It strived to reduce the incidence of anemia and malnutrition among the adolescent girls to break the cycle of ill-health and infant mortality.

13.12 Twelfth Five Year Plan (2012-17): Faster, Sustainable and More Inclusive Growth

The twelfth plan was titled "Faster, Sustainable and More Inclusive growth." It is widely believed that men enjoy all the power, position and privileges and women were treated as second rate and lower humans. The theory of patriarchy puts the question of women in a proper perspective. The Planning Commission pushed for a special dispensation for single women, particularly those who are single by choice, under various government schemes in the 12th five-year plan. In addition to reserving a certain percentage of jobs for single women under centrally sponsored schemes, the plan has proposed promoting and strengthening federations of single women at the block and district level. While the Ministry of Women and Child Development has been taken on board on this, Ministries and States will be asked to add a gender component into their schemes. In framing policies/schemes for the 12th five year plan, the special needs of women must be taken due care of. The Mahila Kisan Sahakatikaran Pariyojana (MKSP), which is a sub-component of NRLM (National Rural Health Mission) was launched to meet the specific attention that needs to be given to leverage the enormous potential of empowering rural women in the rural farm and rural non-farm sector.

14. Entrepreneurship Policy: National Policy for Entrepreneurship

Though several initiatives are in place to promote entrepreneurship in the country, the efforts are disjointed. There is a plethora of policies such as Micro, Small and Medium Enterprise Policy, Manufacturing Policy, Competition Policy, Industrial policy, Science and Technology Policy, National Design Policy, etc., that touch upon and have implications for entrepreneurship, directly and indirectly. But the focus on entrepreneurship remains fragmented and devoid of any strategic content. It is argued that there must be a mechanism in place that leads to a high rate of inflow of new entrepreneurs who in turn create new enterprises. The questions being raised are of the quality and quantity of entrepreneurs who could take advantage of the emerging opportunities in the wake of liberalisation and globalisation of the economies. India unfortunately is deficient on both counts. Across the world, business processes have undergone a sea change in the post liberalisation era. It would be difficult to meet the level of competition with traditional family owned business processes. There is a need to modernise businesses so that they become globally competitive. Entrepreneurship needs to be made a revolution. Therefore, the government has decided to refocus on promotion of entrepreneurship in the country, in a strategic manner, through a comprehensive 'National Entrepreneurship Policy'. (edii.org)

The overall objective of the 'National Entrepreneurship Policy' is to create conducive conditions that augment continuous flow and emergence of opportunity driven entrepreneurs. The specific objectives of the Policy are to:

- Trigger an entrepreneurial culture and inculcate entrepreneurial values in society at large and influence the mind-set of people towards entrepreneurship;

- Create awareness about the charms of being an entrepreneur and the process of entrepreneurship, especially among youth;
- Encourage more dynamic start-ups by motivating educated youth, scientists and technologists to consider entrepreneurship as a lucrative, preferred and viable career;
- Support early phase of entrepreneurship development including the prestart-up, nascent as well as early post start-up phase and growth enterprises;
- Broaden the base of entrepreneurial supply by meeting specific needs of underrepresented target groups like women, minorities, socially and economically backward communities, scheduled castes and scheduled tribes and underrepresented regions to achieve inclusive, balanced and sustainable growth of entrepreneurship in the country;
- Facilitate creation of social enterprises to address the needs of the population at the 'bottom of the pyramid';
- Ensure adequate availability and flow of information to potential entrepreneurs, eliminate entry and exit barriers, create a business friendly, non-threatening and conducive regulatory and policy environment to reduce administrative burden related to compliances of various kinds; and
- Create an eco-system by evolving an institutional framework and organisational structure to achieve the above objectives. (edii.org)
- To achieve the above stated objectives, the government will follow a multipronged strategy:
- Sensitising, Promoting and Igniting Entrepreneurship
- Creating and Fostering Entrepreneurship
- Nurturing Entrepreneurship
- Recognising and Celebrating Entrepreneurship
- Institutionalising the Entrepreneurship Movement. (edii.org).

15. Inclusive Growth in India

In India, it is perceived that a woman's primary role is as a homemaker. Thus, there are a low number of women in gainful employment, which has been further declining, leading to gender wage gaps and limited or no access to productive resources. This enhances economic inequality and impedes the 'access to full citizenship' (Kessler-Harris, 2003). Inappropriate allocation of talent and human capital impacts growth rate of GDR.

In improving women's participation by 10 percentage points, India could add USD 1 billion by 2025 to its GDP.

15.1 Active Role of Government for Financial Empowerment

The government has initiated the Beti Bachao Beti Padhao Programme that addresses the complex issue of mindsets in all districts of India. If people are not made to change the way they think about girls and women, we are unlikely to see much long-lasting success in other initiatives for empowerment.

Economic empowerment is central to the overall empowerment of women, and financial inclusion is an important part of this. For instance, a few years ago, opening a bank account was considered a tedious task. But through the Sukanya Samriddhi Yojana and PM Jan Dhan Yojana, Government has enabled banking services for the unbanked. 16.42 crore women's accounts have been opened under Jan Dhan. Women's share of total savings accounts increased from 28 percent in 2014 to 40 percent in 2017 (according to the data from top 40 banks and RRBs). This is a sizeable and rapid growth in financial inclusion of women, a cherished goal for decades.

15.2 Empowering Motherhood

To retain women in the workforce, the Maternity Benefit Act has been amended to extend the period of mandatory paid maternity leave for working women to 26 weeks. This empowers working women as they need not fear loss of salary or job due to childbirth and now they also have time to recuperate and breastfeed their child.

In order to extend protection to the unorganised sector as well, pregnant and lactating mothers are provided cash incentives under the PM Matru Vandana Yojana. As partial compensation for wage loss, these mothers are provided ₹ 6,000 as incentive, which enables them to take adequate rest before and after the delivery and exclusively breastfeed their child. Over 38 lakh beneficiaries are already enrolled under this scheme.

15.3 Empowering Women: Legal Provisions

Empowering women to make their own decisions without any limitations and treating them at par with men is imperative for the holistic progress of the nation. Our Constitution guarantees the right to equality and the right not to be discriminated against on the basis of sex. However, gender discrimination has its roots in the Indian society since ancient times.

The right to property and the right of women to own property has also been the subject-matter of interpretation of the Courts, judicial pronouncements, amendments and statutory enactments. The amendment to the Hindu Succession Act, 1956 gave women the right to a share in the joint family property of both, the parents and the in-laws. Prior to this, women had a right to a limited estate. The ouster of women of women from right to inherent and own property, if they married outside the community, is present under tribal law as well as religious. Under Chotanagpur Tenancy Act, 1908, who married outside the community, were said to have "lost their right to parental property."

15.4 Uniform Civil Code

The preamble of the Constitution of India states that "We, the People of India, having solemnly resolved to constitute India into a Sovereign Socialist Secular Democratic Republic and..." Secularism means equal treatment of all the religions by the State. A Uniform Civil Code which governs the personal matters of all the citizens irrespective of their religion is the linchpin of true secularism. There is a need for such a code as various personal laws prevalent in India discriminate against women and have a long way to move towards promoting gender parity. With the increase in the number of women approaching the Courts to protect their fundamental rights, the law Commission has been asked to probe into possibility of implementation of the Uniform Civil Code in India, whereby men and the women will be put at par in relation to personal laws.

15.5 Power of Communication: Social Interaction and Social Change

Communication has an overarching role in human society. It unleashes a process of social interaction through various modes for exchange of information-verbal, non-verbal, words in print or audio-visual format. Modern technology-enabled society with the help of mass media is making the best use of the power of communication in ameliorating the lives of people. The amalgamation of human lives and mass media in the present era has given rise to a tremendous force in stimulating a sense of involvement among masses, an essential prerequisite for transformation in society.

The growth in ICT has further boosted the scope and outreach of communication coverage and enhanced opportunities for education, both formal and informal, skill development, capacity-building, financial inclusion, healthcare, etc.

The recent policy statements bear a mark of the nation's persistent determination to reach the goals of inclusivity and empowerment. The National Policy for Women (NPW), 2016, is a landmark document, which pronounces the resolve realising the constructive engagement of women in nation development. The Sexual Harassment of Women at Workplace (Prevention, Prohibition and Redressal) Act, 2013, is a path breaking law, enforcing an obligation upon every employer for ensuring a safe working space. The Act specifically emphasizes sensitisation of employees about the safeguards provided in it for women's safety. Our country continues to progress towards achieving the goal of women having increased economic independence and acquiring means for self-sustenance. The recently launched Pradhan Mantri Jan Dhan Yojana, has within two years brought in 16.34 crore women under the banking system, and in terms of new accounts openings, women have stolen a march on men. Similarly, under the Sukanya Samruddhi Yojana which is an attempt to secure future of a girl child, more than 1.26 crore new accounts have been opened in the name of girl children up to November, 2017, within two years of its launch. Women again far surpassed men in garnering more than 75 percent of sanctioned loans under the Mudra scheme for entrepreneurship development. There is no doubt that mass media has played a critical role in yielding beneficial results from the schemes for women's empowerment and in highlighting the issues of gender rights to a larger audience base.

The immense power of communication and new technologies has indeed triggered a motivation for enhanced participation and also generated an urge in articulating a demand for change. Today, the majority of women are in a position to fight for their rightful place in society. This newly earned and much needed confidence will go a long way in heralding a new era for women's multifaceted development.

15.6 Safety in Workplace

An important aspect of empowerment is also safety. Only if women feel safe and secure they will be able to fully participate in the economy and public life. For this, the government has sanctioned Women Helplines in States/ UTs and 206 One Stop Centres have become operational where women affected by violence can access quick and easy help. 33 percent reservation for women in the police force is also being implemented. The Nirbhaya Fund is also being used to roll-out comprehensive plans to make 8 major cities in the country safer for women and also improve our forensic analysis abilities in cases of sexual assault. All these and many other initiatives for safety will support the empowerment journey of women (yojana.org).

16. Schemes for Economic Development

The National Scheduled Tribes Finance and Development Corporation is an apex organisation under Ministry of Tribal Affairs for economic development of STs. The Corporation is having an exclusive scheme for economic development of ST women titled "Adivasi Mahila Sashaktikaran Yojana" (AMSY). Under the scheme, the Corporation provides financial assistance upto 90 percent to projects with an outlay of Rs I lakh at a concessional rate of interest of 4 percent. The Corporation also extends its financial assistance for women beneficiaries under other income generating schemes. (Ministry of Tribal affairs)

16.1 Right to Forest Produce

The Scheduled Tribes and Other Traditional Forest Dwellers (Recognition of Forest Rights) Act, provides for full and unrestricted participation of women at all levels. Another important provision in the Act is that the "right conferred shall be registered jointly in the name of both the spouses".

The Forest Rights Committee provides that at least two-third members shall be Scheduled Tribes and not less than one-third of such members shall be women.

Under the scheme of Special Central Assistance to Tribal Sub Scheme (SCA to TSS) and Grants under Article 275 (1) of the Constitution skill development and capacity building of ST women are taken up by States with complete support of MoTA. The Tribal Research Institutes conduct training cum awareness programmes and workshops for ST women Panchayati Raj Institutions (PRI) members on several issues like leadership development, women empowerment, awareness on PESA, FRA etc. Steps are also being taken to improve the infrastructure in tribal areas including road connectivity, modernisation of tribal haats (markets), improving the processing and storage facilities, etc. MoTA has encouraged tribal festivals at National and State levels that serve as window for tribals including women folk to showcase rich skills and talents in varied art forms.

16.2 Schemes on NWDES

Training of Rural Youth for Self-Employment (TRYSEM)

(1) The Scheme of TRYSEM, a facilitating component of IRDP, aims at providing basic technical and entrepreneurial skills to the rural

poor in the age group of 18 to 35 years to enable them to take up income generating activities. The Eighth Plan had emphasized the importance of a proper assessment of the training needs of the rural youth in relation to self and wage-employment opportunities, quality of training and group training. During the Eighth Plan, 15.28 lakh youth were trained under TRYSEM, of whom 34.16 percent took up self-employment and 15.05 percent wage-employment; while the remaining 50.79 percent remained unemployed.

With a view to strengthening this programme, several initiatives were taken which include an increase in the stipend and honorarium rates; emphasis on professionals training through the established and recognised institutes like ITIs, Community Polytechnics, Krishi Vigyan Kendras etc., exploring the possibilities of setting up production groups from amongst TRYSEM trainees for undertaking ancillary activities.

(2) Prime Ministers Rojgar Yojana (PMRY)

PMRY is being implemented since 1993. The Scheme is designed to create and provide sustainable self-employment opportunities to one million educated unemployed youth in the country during the 8th Plan period. It was also felt that certain parameters of the PMRY Scheme need modification. For example, condition of eligibility such as age, educational qualifications was coming in the way of expanding the coverage of the scheme in some cases. Similarly the total financial assistance per case was found to be insufficient in case of certain viable activities.

(3) Entrepreneurial Development Programme (EDP)

EDP is a program meant to develop entrepreneurial abilities among the people. It refers to inculcation, development, and polishing of entrepreneurial skills into a person needed to establish and successfully run his / her enterprise. Thus, the concept of entrepreneurship development programme involves equipping a person with the required skills and knowledge needed for starting and running the enterprise.

(4) The Working Women's Forum

The Working Women's Forum (WWF) is a women's organisation in southern India. It was founded in 1978 by Jaya Arunachalam in Madras (Chennai). The WWF aims to empower poor women in southern India by providing microcredits, a trade union, health care and training. It works with the poor women working in the informal sector, such as street vendors, silkworm growers and silk weavers, handicraft producers, washerwomen and fisherwomen.

(5) Mahila Samridhi Yojana

Providing micro finance for targeted women belonging to the backward classes as notified by Central / State Govt. from time to time. The annual family income of the women is fixed as ₹ 3.00 Lakh. The SCAs/Banks are requested to release at least 50% of total funding to persons with annual family income upto ₹ 1.50 Lakh.

(6) The Rajiv Gandhi Mahila Vikas Pariyojana (RGMVP)

The Rajiv Gandhi Mahila Vikas Pariyojana (RGMVP) is the flagship programme of Rajiv Gandhi Charitable Trust, a registered non-profit institution, working for poverty reduction, women empowerment and rural development in Uttar Pradesh, India since 2002. RGMVP believes that "the poor have a strong desire and innate ability to overcome poverty". It aims to organise poor rural women into community institutions and promotes financial inclusion, healthcare, livelihood enhancement, education and environment.

(7) Micro Credit Scheme

Creating self-employment opportunities is one way of attacking poverty and solving the problems of unemployment. There are over 24 core people below the poverty line in the country. The Scheme of Micro-Credit has been found as an effective instrument for lifting the poor above the level of poverty by providing them increased self-employment opportunities and making them credit worthy. Total requirement of micro-credit in the country has been assessed at ₹ 50, 000 crore. Micro-credit programme works through NGOs/SHGs and the merit lies in weekly monitoring and refund of installments. The rate of recovery under SIDBI's Micro credit programme is as high as 98%. Though there are various Departments and Organisations implementing micro-credit schemes in the areas of activity falling under their purview but their total reach is very low i.e. not more than ₹ 5,000 crore. Thus, the existing programme cater to only 5 to 10% of total requirements and there is considerable scope for expansion of such programmes.

(8) Rashtriya Mahila Kosh

Rashtriya Mahila Kosh (RMK) was established by the Government of India in March, 1993 as an autonomous body under the Ministry of Women & Child Development. It was registered under the Societies Registration Act 1860.

Objectives of RMK Establishment

RMK is a national level organisation as an autonomous body under the aegis of the Ministry of Women and Child Development, for socioeconomic empowerment of women. The operating model currently followed by RMK is that of a facilitating agency wherein RMK provides loans to NGO-MFIs termed as Intermediary Organisations (IMO) which on-lend to Self Help Groups (SHGs) of women.

- This scheme is for providing loans to new and smaller organisations with experience of at least 6 months in thrift & credit. The organisation can avail a maximum loan up to ₹ 10 lakhs.
- RMK extends micro-credit to the needy and poor women in the informal sector through a client friendly, without collateral and in a hassle-free manner for livelihood activities, housing, micro-enterprises, family needs, etc. RMK has taken a number of promotional measures to popularize the concept of micro financing, thrift and credit, formation and stabilisation of SHGs and also enterprise development for poor women through intermediary organisations working at grass root level such as Non - governmental organisations, Women Federations, Co-operatives, Urban Women Cooperative Banks, Government Autonomous Bodies, not for profit-Section 25 companies registered under Companies Act, and all other Voluntary / Civil Society Organisations etc.
- This scheme is for providing loans to organisations having minimum 3 years' experience in thrift & credit activities. The organisation can avail a maximum loan upto 2 crores for 1 state. An organisation can avail loan under the scheme for a maximum number of 3 states at a time. If the organisation avails loan for more than 1 state, then the maximum loan amount can be upto ₹ 6 crores.
- This scheme is for providing bulk loans to medium and large NGOs. This scheme is meant for organisation which has in the past availed loan from RMK and have not defaulted in repayment. The organisation can avail a maximum loan upto ₹ 5 crores.

- This scheme is for providing loan for construction/ repair and maintenance of houses to women who are members of Self Help Group/ Joint Liability Groups (JLGs). This loan is provided through IMOs/NGOs/VOs. The organisation can avail a maximum loan up to ₹ 1, 00,000 per beneficiary for construction of low cost house. The organisation has to mortgage the immovable property created out of RMK's loan by deposit of title deed (i.e. equitable mortgage). The NGO/ IMO/VO may hold the deeds in trust for RMK and details of the same be captured in RMK database. An NGO/IMO/ VO can avail a maximum loan upto ₹ 6 crores for a maximum of 3 states at a time.
- Organisations availing loan from RMK shall on-lend to the end beneficiaries for income generating activities such as setting up of small business, asset creation, agriculture, petty shop, livestock rearing, transport services, etc.

(9) SIDBI Mahila Udyam Nidhi

SIDBI Mahila Udyam Nidhi is designed to help meet gap in equity in startups by women entrepreneurs. SIDBI or Small Industries Development Bank of India is the principal financial institution for the promotion, financing and development of industry in the small scale sector. The purpose of Mahila Udyam Nidhi is to help women entrepreneurs meeting equity funds requirement will setting up a new business.

(10) Stree Shakti Package for Women Entrepreneurs

There is a lot of focus on promoting women entrepreneurship in India with the government and financial institutions having various schemes. One such scheme promoted by the State Bank of India (SBI) is Stree Shakti Package for Women Entrepreneurs.

(11) SEWA bank project

SEWA is a trade union registered in 1972. It is an organisation of poor, self-employed women workers. These are women who earn a living through their own labour or small businesses. They do not obtain regular salaried employment with welfare benefits like workers in the organised sector. They are the unprotected labour force of our country. Constituting 93% of the labour force, these are workers of the unorganised sector. Of the female labour force in India, more than 94% are in the unorganised sector. However their work is not counted and hence remains invisible.

(12) Micro & small enterprises cluster development Programme

The Ministry of Micro, Small and Medium Enterprises (MSME), Government of India (GoI) has adopted the Cluster Development approach as a key strategy for enhancing the productivity and competitiveness as well as capacity building of Micro and Small Enterprises (MSEs) and their collectives in the country. A cluster is a group of enterprises located within an identifiable and as far as practicable, contiguous area and producing same / similar products/services.

(13) Pradhan Mantri Mahila Kendra

Government of India has approved a new scheme namely, Pradhan Mantri Mahila Shakti Kendra (MSK) for 2017-18 upto 2019-20 to empower rural women through community participation and to create an environment in which they realize their full potential.

The new scheme is envisaged to work at various levels. While, National level (domain based knowledge support) and State level (State Resource Centre for Women) structures will provide technical support to the respective government on issues related to women, the District and Block level Centres will provide support to MSK and also give a foothold to BBBP in 640 districts to be covered in a phased manner.

(14) The Rajiv Gandhi Mahila Vikas Pariyojana (RGMVP)

The Rajiv Gandhi Mahila Vikas Pariyojana (RGMVP) is the flagship programme of Rajiv Gandhi Charitable Trust, a registered non-profit institution, working for poverty reduction, women empowerment and rural development in Uttar Pradesh, India since 2002. RGMVP believes that "the poor have a strong desire and innate ability to overcome poverty". It aims to organize poor rural women into community institutions and promotes financial inclusion, health-care, livelihood enhancement, education and environment.

Key Ideas of the Chapter

Gender mainstreaming exercise has been a process of learning and refinement throughout the planning process. The First to Fifth Five Year Plans treated the development of women as a subject of 'welfare'. The Central Social Welfare Board (CSWB) was set up during 1953 to promote welfare-oriented activities for women and children at the grassroot level. The welfare approach continued during this period, priority was also given to women's education and maternal and child health services.

'Women welfare' to 'women development' was promoted during the Sixth Plan. The Sixth Plan had special thrust on the three core sectors viz., health, education, and employment. The Seventh Plan was continued with the developmental approach. The major objective of seventh plan was of raising the economic and social status of women and bringing them into the mainstream of national development. Human development was a significant focus of the Eighth Plan for ensuring that women were not bypassed from the benefits of various developmental programmes.

Empowerment of Women as Agents of Social Change and Development was continued in the Tenth Plan. Towards this a Sector-specific 3-Fold Strategy was adopted based on the National Policy for Empowerment of Women.

The conceptual framework for analysing gender was focused on three domains of gender equality: endowments, particularly health, education and social protection; economic opportunity. These three pillars are strongly interconnected. Health and education contribute to women's ability to take advantage of economic opportunities and to their capacity to exercise voice and agency.

The success of a country in empowering women is highly dependent on the responsive and multifaceted approach to public policy management and implementation, including its macro-economic, financial and trade policies.

The details about gender budgeting is discussed in the chapter. The primary driving force for proposing gender budgeting is the need to highlight the marginalisation of women in policies. Gender budgeting refers to the presentation of budgetary data in a manner so that the gender sensitivities of the budgetary allocations are highlighted.

Gender budgeting was included in all the strategic important departments including Science & Technology, Department of Biotechnology, Information Technology, Labour, Youth Affairs, Panchayati Raj, Human Resource Development, Health and Family Welfare and Rural Development. Among the key objectives, priority is being accorded to providing support to women for gender parity in Science & Technology.

The National Commission for Women is a national level statutory body was also set up in 1990 to work towards safeguarding the rights and interests of women and thus has been working towards gender justice for women in the country. The principal activities of the Commission were investigation, examination, and review of all matters relating to safeguards provided to women under the Indian Constitution. Women related legislation and to suggest suitable amendments were made keeping surveillance and facilitating redressal of grievances of women, etc. The twelfth Plan was titled "Faster, Sustainable and More Inclusive growth." It is widely believed that men enjoy all the power, position and privileges and women were treated as second rate and lower humans. The theory of patriarchy puts the question of women in a proper perspective. The Scheme of Training of Rural Youth for Self-Employment TRYSEM, a facilitating basic technical and entrepreneurial skills to the rural poor in the age group of 18 to 35 years to enable them to take up income generating activities. PMRY is being implemented since 1993. The Scheme is designed to create and provide sustainable self-employment opportunities to one million educated unemployed youth in the country during the 8th Plan period.

The working women's forum (WWF) was founded in 1978 by Jaya Arunachalam in Madras (Chennai). Creating self-employment opportunities is one way of attacking poverty and solving the problems of unemployment. There are over 24 Core people below the poverty line in the country. Pradhan Mantri Mahila Kendra was formulated and applicable for 2017-18 upto 2019-20 to empower rural women through community participation and to create an environment in which they realise their full potential.

Chapter - 4

Gender Gap

1. Female Labour Force Participation in India

In comparison with Brazil, whose two-third of its working-age women have jobs, India's proportion is only one-third. Women's labour force participation is higher in rural areas and Southern regions of India than urban and Northern region. The participation rate may reflect a religious dimension, i.e. in northern regions, the population of Muslims is higher where they tend to have lower female participation rate. (ILO, 2014)

It is also observed that women's participation is more amongst poor and declines with family income and education, although it is higher among the highest educated. In a study of over 100 countries, female labour force participation was found to the first decline with per capita incomes and rise only when women became more educated and had access to white-collar jobs.

Among the BRICS nations, Female Labour Force Participation Rate (FLFPR) is diminishing in China and India, whereas in Brazil, Indonesia and South Africa the rate is reviving. Most of the decline in the female labour force since 2005 is due to a drop in unpaid female self-employment in agriculture. While female working-age population rose by about 99 million, female jobs grew only by 6 million between 2000 and 2012 as employment first rose between 2000-2005 but then declined after that. As a result, the amount of working-age women outside the labour force grew by over 60 million in the past decade. The gap in male-female labour force participation rate amongst emerging markets is highest in India at 50%, followed by Indonesia; the least is in Russia (which is also less than the OECD average). According to the NSSO surveys, many women who stayed at home specified that they like to work regularly either part time or full time, especially if they could work from home. Access to finance, training, and to have an assured market were factors that would facilitate taking up a job.

The best way to eradicate poverty is to adopt the new development model which should be based on Base of Pyramid (BoP), (London and Hart, (2011)). The objectives of the BoP model is to create job opportunity for the people who are at the base of the pyramid involving them in socioeconomic development.

The only way to reduce the gender gap is to promote gender promotional activities in the rural areas by promoting entrepreneurship activity among the women who will have to narrow down the gender gap by reducing poverty and encourage employment generation activity (Schumpeter, 1936). Gender equality plays an essential role in economic development. Various studies have highlighted how lower female labour force participation or weak entrepreneurial activity drags down economic growth, and that empowering woman has significant economic benefits in addition to promoting gender equality (Duflo, 2005; World Bank, 2012).

The report observed that in India and other low-ranked countries, unequal inheritance rights for women and work restrictions limited their access to start-up capital and collateral.

The world will need 600 million jobs by 2025 to employ a qualified workforce. With start-ups generating 70-90% of all new jobs, entrepreneurs represent the answer to that challenge. To meet this demand, it is to ensure that women entrepreneurs should have the opportunity to start and scale their businesses to the same level as their male counterparts.

Five countries receive overall scores in the low range (under 30 out of 100); these countries represent South Asian and MENA countries. In South Asia, the top-ranking country is India, ranked 29th with a score of 17 out of 100.

3. Job Opportunities at the Bottom of the Pyramid

Women also participate economically as entrepreneurs and self-employed. Female entrepreneurs are mostly involved in the services sector than in manufacturing and trading. The growth of self-employed females has doubled between 2000 and 2010. These women work from home in traditional arenas such as textiles, apparel and tobacco while many opt to work as street vendors. The stagnant share of entrepreneurs with often higher education and skills can reflect many remaining barriers for female economic activities such as social norms, or access to credit etc. (Daymard and Sorsa, 2015).

3.1 Stylised Facts for India

Low female labour force participation rate (FLFPR) in India is declining further when compared to any other region in the world. The gap in male-female rates, low and stagnant urban rates and declining rural rates, loss of women from the labour market in all regions and sectors are the primary features. Delhi has 17 percent FLFPR with 24 percent in other metros while Ludhiana has the highest male participation rate (83 per cent) but a mere 12 percent FLFPR.

More women are available for additional work and report augmenting income as an important reason for this. Aspirations and need for employment are still high among women with unemployment rates (UR) being higher than men. The principal status of male UR has remained around 2-3 percent (3-4 per cent) in rural (urban) while the female current daily status of UR is around 3-4 percent in rural and varying between 7-9 percent in urban.

FWPR declines with education and slightly increases at very high levels and is more apparent in 2011 than in 2005, and more in metros followed by non-metro cities. For any education category, the usual status of UR for women is higher by 2-5 percentage points in 2011-12 and high rural rates of 17-18 percent (only 4-5 percent for men) among higher secondary and diploma holders.

According to the (Deloitte report) titled Empowering Women & Girls in India for the Fourth Industrial Revolution, 95 percent or 195 million women are employed in the unorganised sector or are in unpaid work. The female labour force participation in India fell to 26 percent in 2018 from 36.7 percent in 2005; reasons might be the lack of access to quality education and underlying social, economic barriers limiting the opportunities for women.

Nature of employment varies across regions, types and sector of the industry. Women in Northern states have lower FWPR compared to Southern states; more women are in subsidiary status employment in both rural and urban areas, and they predominate in the agricultural sector. The next largest FWPR is in public services where the state is the primary employer, followed by one segment of manufacturing industries like the textile sector.

3.2 Determinants of FWPR

Demand-side or structural factors and supply-side or cultural factors like family roles and societal norms impact FWPR. The role of caregiving and the limited time spent by men in sharing the household work are primary factors depressing FWPR and studies have shown that with domestic help or presence of informal support from other family members improves FWPR.

Thirty percent reservation in government jobs in some states (Assam, Gujarat, Karnataka, Maharashtra and Tamil Nadu) did not seem to have a significant impact with public jobs shrinking. As part of corporate governance policies all over the world, India instituted quotas for women in the board since 2013. The increased presence of women improves the firm's value and performance, but this could be affected by the nature of control in family firms.

Better responsiveness of the state to crime rates and sexual harassment, laws extending night working hours for women and incentives for women entrepreneurs, impacts inter-state variation in FWPR. Chances of participation in the workforce for women increases in regions where there is higher reported confidence in police/ judiciary and lower reported crime.

China and India could reap significant gains from promoting gender equality and female participation in the workforce.

3.3 Women in Work Index

In recent decades, rapid economic growth in both these countries has led to significant improvements in female economic empowerment. The analysis suggests that further efforts to promote gender equality and female participation in the workforce could generate significant gains for both economic powerhouses, India would rank at the bottom of the index, which is not surprising given its relatively lower state of economic development compared to OECD countries. India faces a significant challenge with a relatively large gender pay gap of 36%, significantly higher than any of the other countries included in the Index. Closing the gender pay gap would generate a 56% increase in female earnings, equivalent to a $245 billion boost to female earnings. India struggles with low levels of female participation in the workforce due in part to prevailing cultural norms about the role of women in society.

4. Government Initiative for Promoting FWPR

With the expansion of NRHM, ASHA workers have increased, impacting FWPR. Alongside the ICDS the Creche schemes had been strengthened. Further, in these two schemes, women would be the service providers which could make widespread additions to the workforce across all rural India. Additional allocation of 173 crores for Women in public transport in the 2018 Union Budget and similarly, subsidised scooter scheme for working women in Tamil Nadu are essential steps. Hostel for Working Women Scheme was brought in as an effort towards creating a safe working environment and providing affordable accommodation for working women away from their hometown.

The Maternity Benefit Act, 1961 was amended in 2017 (Maternity Benefit Amendment Bill 2017) to primarily include increased paid maternity leave from 12 to 26 weeks, provide an option of 'work from home' for women after the 26 weeks and also included the provision of creche facility and leave for mothers adopting children. The amendment would cover the organised sector, and with no provisions for women in the unorganised sector, its implications are yet to be analyzed.

5. Existence of Problems and Reasons

Women still contribute a disproportionate amount of unpaid work in their homes and on farms. Despite having more control over their finances, they are often not given an equal say in household or work decisions. These are the stark realities of life even now. This continuing discrimination and violence need to be recognised and acted upon if we want to see true empowerment of the Indian woman.

5.1 Gender Participation Gaps

There is a growing literature on the economic implications of gender participation gaps (summarised in IMF, 2013). The literature stresses that gender gaps in labour force participation, entrepreneurial activity, or education act to impede economic growth (Esteve-Volart, 2004, and Klasen and Lamanna, 2008).

Cuberes and Teigner (2014) examine the quantitative effects of gender gaps in labour force participation on productivity and living standards. They simulate an occupational choice model with heterogeneous agents that imposes several frictions on female economic participation and their wages and shows that gender gaps in entrepreneurship and labour force participation significantly reduce per capita income. For India, they find that gender gaps lower overall per worker incomes by about 26 percent.

Agenor (2015) uses an overlapping generations model in three phases, including childhood, working and retirement. He suggested stimulating the effect of public policies (including public investment in infrastructure and efficiency of spending on health and education) on participation choices and economic growth (via impact on human capital, productivity and labour input directly).

Different departments like central government, state governments have adopted this programme to accelerate the process of organising the poor, especially the women into the SHGs. Further, NRLM has adopted the programme from the SGSY as a flagship programme to promote minimum one woman from the low-income family into the SHG group. Other, microcredit programme, play an essential role in the financial system in India, besides longer being part of the programme has shown a positive impact on the consumption level, nutrition level and in asset accumulation.

5.2. Equality of Laws and Economic Opportunities

In several countries, the government accountability on gender is limited, and often there is a lack of awareness about public services and the capacity to assess the impact of the policy of men and women. The agencies which work for gender equality have a low profile, and thus the availability of gender-disaggregated data can be an issue.

In India, with the introduction of gender budget, the reporting of allocation of the budget has become much more straightforward. Studies have shown that with affirmative action and quotas for women for political representation; they can voice their opinion in a much more effective way. It has also increased the likelihood of women being engaged in the labour force. Participation in the workforce is possibly influenced by the significant wage differential faced by women in India, thus forcing women to stay at home. It is especially observed among unskilled workers who are hardly literate. The legal framework for equal pay is not always enforced (Equal Remuneration Act of 1976), partly reflecting the large share of the informal sector (about 95% of employment).

6. Factors Affecting Women Participation

(i) Wage differentials, education, and income

These dimensions have a strong presence in South and Western regions of India which have a more female population and higher female participation as compared to East and North-east where the female participation is low due to cultural and traditional factors. Though there is a short-term reduction in female participation, over time, socio-economic factors will be countered by education. Education is also one of the strongest determinants of female entrepreneurship in India (Daymard and Sorsa, 2015) because it assists them in building human capital, the required skills and experience. (ILO, 2014)

(ii) Wealth

Wealth can affect the involvement of women in the labour force when sources of permanent income are available, and when it is beyond total earnings and socio-economic status. Wealth often reduces the necessity to work, apart from perhaps at the highest levels of education. Studies endorse that an increase in unearned income of the household reduces the marginal utility of the woman's earnings and thereby participation.

(iii) Social institutions and inequality

In India, the cultural obstacle for women's participation primarily comes through the patriarchal system, which is often against women's economic freedom. Religious attitudes determine women's economic participation. Additionally, it also influenced by social class. In traditional societies, risks of exposure to other males outside the home has reduced female participation. Thus, self-employment within the home may be a way to reduce those social risks while raising participation in the labour force. India ranks low on the OECD, SIGI index measuring social obstacles to gender equality and a World Bank index on governance.

(iv) Infrastructure as an economic barrier to participation

Infrastructure such as roads, technology, access to water and electricity, safety and availability are few factors which can be positively used to enhance women participation. These factors also contribute to bolstering women entrepreneurship.

(v) Education reduces socio-economic barriers to participation

Education brings several benefits to women where they are in the position to make decisions on their own and take advantage of economic opportunities. Education has complex socio-economic linkages related to female well-being. Girls access to education is influenced by marriage age, which in some parts of India is low.

Over the years, much progress has been made to enhance the school enrolment of girls at the primary level. Nevertheless, more efforts have to made to further the reach of the girls to take a quality secondary and higher education. A high unemployment rate is observed in higher educated women due to skill mismatch issues.

The bias between male and female begins at an early age in very subtle ways, and it is crucial to solve early paths of inequality that is more difficult and costly to resolve over time.

In India, many laws have been formulated to protect women's rights and guarantee them equal treatment. However, traditional and religious customs often take precedence. Traditional/religious customs like son preference, dowry, no equal pays.

(vi) Institutions and access to resources

Some laws and regulations such as those which forbid women from working at night or in certain occupations, limit their job opportunities thus, migrating them to jobs in agriculture and informal sector as self-employed.

(vii) Lack of social protection can influence participation

The formal sector has benefitted from several social protection schemes such as Payment of Gratuity, pension schemes, provident funds etc. Several measures have been introduced to facilitate labour participation to give social protection for women in the informal sector.

(viii) Availability of care

Prevalence of unpaid work is mostly attributed to the lack of affordable care facilities. Lack of care facilities for children and elderly persons from the family often results in lower participation in the labour force. However, having more females in the household may raise participation because another female relative may take care of the children and the elderly.

(ix) Active labour market policies

There is a need for effective active labour market policies which should aim at reducing market and institutional failures affecting female employment. For instance, rural public employment programmes (NREG) recommends that 33 percent of jobs be reserved for women as such programmes help raise the female labour force participation.

Skill development programmes have also been proven effective to make a difference. In India, one such programme is STEP which is initiated by the Ministry of Women and Child Development for assestless rural and urban women. Also, the private sector should be encouraged to hire women at all levels.

(x) Entrepreneurship policies

The active training programmes have led to an increase in the number of female entrepreneurs in the manufacturing and services industry. Additionally, female entrepreneurship can also be facilitated by promoting role models and networks.

Networks and agglomeration bring positive location externalities for production and market opportunities, which can help to boost productivity and lower unit costs (Fujita et al., 1999; Ghani *et al.*, 2012) unless overtaken by congestion costs.

(xi) Access to finance

Women with access to pension and savings in bank accounts are more capable of making independent decisions on resource use. Enhancing women's control over the resources increases their bargaining power in households (Duflo, 2012). There is also a strong relationship between women's financial inclusion and their performance as entrepreneurs in developing countries (OECD, 2012). Financial inclusion is considered as an important tool to lessen the poverty by promoting entrepreneurship, creation of jobs.

To improve access to finance for women, numerous schemes have been introduced Rashtriya Mahila Kosh, NABARD Schemes, etc. Many studies have suggested that microcredit is used for consumption and not for productive investment. Access to credit for women for productive purposes can be enhanced by measures enabling collateralisation of loans with cash flow or equipment. Discriminatory loan practices whereby men sign women's documents in banks should be eliminated in law. Other options are to strengthen credit bureaus and other institutions that collect info on borrowers.

7. Raising Women's Participation Contribute in Growth Effects

A more rigorous assessment of potential growth, gains of higher participation and the interaction of various determinants were made with overlapping generation models. The time use of women was modelled over three periods (childhood, adulthood and retirement) in an economy that produces home and market goods. The model was used to simulate public policies that affect female time use, and thereby economic participation and potential growth. The policies include changes in public investment in infrastructure, such as safer and better transport, sanitation and water; the efficiency of government spending in health, education and infrastructure to the extent they impact women's time allocation. The model is also used to simulate the impact of the child- and gender-related policies such as increasing family benefits per child, reducing gender bias in the marketplace and mother's time allotted to daughters on participation. These policies raise growth by improving human and other capital, productivity and labour input lifting the economy to a new steady state with a permanently higher growth rate (Agenor, 2015).

7.1. Reasons for Low Participation of Women in the Workforce

- Inequalities in opportunities which arise due the time use differences between men and women that keeps women out of the labour force.
- Women generally handle domestic duties.
- Unequal access to productive inputs such as credit and labour, and market and institutional failures.
- Biased social norms Gender-differentiated market failures, institutional constraints, and persistent social norms often combine to reinforce gender inequalities and make improving gender equality much more complicated. There are multiple constraints and all the constraints need to be addressed through well-designed policy and its application process (World Bank, 2012).

The reasons for the low participation of females in India are complicated as there exist large differences across regions and include both supply and demand factors. Supply of female labour is influenced by socio-economic and cultural factors, access to resources, safety concerns with infrastructure, biases in regulations or income levels. Thus, to raise the participation of female in the labour force requires a robust policy that deals with the supply concerns. Additionally, it also requires the creation of job opportunities for women which can be delivered by macroeconomic and structural policies that create new investment.

(i) Challenge in Reaching the Poorest of the Poor and Women in Remote Communities

The challenge is to reach poor women who are landless labourers, smallholder agricultural producers, cross - border traders and factory and domestic workers and ensure that these women have access to the opportunities and benefits of economic growth and trade. There are many challenges when working with the women such as lower levels of literacy, lower levels of access to and control over resources, lower levels of access to networks and people who can assist and support, greater vulnerability to sexual exploitation and abuse at the community level.

(ii) Micro-credit challenge

Micro-finance – including micro-credits – is often considered as an instrument that promotes empowerment. While it can stabilise livelihoods, broaden choices, provide start-up funds for productive investment, help poor people to smooth consumption flows and send children to school, it can also lead to indebtedness and increased exclusion unless programmes are well - designed. Banks in developing countries often have conservative lending practices. Consequently, small women-owned businesses face difficulties accessing the credit needed to invest in expanding their activities. Innovative interventions have encouraged the finance sector to deliver gender-responsive products.

(iii) Reaching the poorest of the poor and women in remote communities

The challenge is to reach poor women who are landless labourers, smallholder agricultural producers, cross - border traders and factory and domestic workers and ensure that these women have access to the opportunities and benefits of economic growth and trade. There are specific challenges when working with the poorest women such as lower levels of literacy, lower levels of access to and control over resources, lower levels of access to networks and people who can assist and support, greater vulnerability to sexual exploitation and abuse at the community level, if not the household level support to the female farmer and her husband. As farmers, processors and traders, women, supply local, regional and international markets with a wide range of goods. The enduring perception of farmers as male – in the face of all evidence to the contrary – is an essential obstacle to the improvement of agricultural production and productivity. The persistence of gender inequalities directly results in poorer agricultural and human development outcomes.

8. Gender and Microenterprise Development

(i) Women and MSME

In general, there are two types of businesswomen, those who choose entrepreneurship and those for whom entrepreneurship is the only option for earning an income (European Commission 1998). Both types of entrepreneurs are increasing in number, the first due to the glass-ceiling effect, and the second in response to increasing unemployment and decreasing wages (Turner, 1993; European Commission, 1998; OECD, 1998b).

A rationale for targeting women MSE owners is welfare improvement. MSE agencies with socially oriented goals, including poverty alleviation, can use the numbers to justify women's inclusion. If MSEs have a role in poverty alleviation, and women play a significant role in the sector as well as in providing for the household, then including them in programmes to promote microenterprise development is justified.

Another rationale for intervening to support women in the MSE sector is to contribute to their social and economic empowerment. Entrepreneurship promotion agencies support this rationale with the belief that self-employment and entrepreneurship increase women's self-esteem and confidence, leading to greater control over their lives in social and economic spheres. This can benefit both women and their families. While these three rationales may be 'true', in that economic growth, poverty alleviation and women's social and economic empowerment potentially can result from women's inclusion in the MSE sector, how women are also included very important.

(ii) Empowering the Nation With Women-Led Development

Over the years, nation have increasingly seen women grow in public life — working in offices, representing India on the international sports arena, in bureaucracy, politics, international organisations and much more. This change is positive and it is happening at a pace faster than ever before.

The recent developments in the area of women empowerment are extremely encouraging. The first female fighter pilot have recently been appointed in the Indian Air Force. The participation of women in combat roles in the Army is also firmly under consideration. The Olympics, Commonwealth Games, and several international sporting events including cricket have seen outstanding performances by Indian women. Even India's successful launch of the Mangalyaan and the record-breaking 104 Nanosatellites launched into orbit onboard a single rocket had a team of women scientists behind them.

These women are role models for a country, which now echoes with the slogan of 'Beti Bachao Beti padhao. India has been prosperous in achieving gender parity in school education. Even in technical and professional education such as medicine, law, IT, engineering, management, etc., the representation of women is significantly increasing. The literacy rate of women has risen from a mere 9 percent in 1951 to 65 percent in 2011. This, in itself, is a considerable turnaround factor.

In the workplace today, every fourth worker in India is a woman. The more technical and complicated the work, the more likely we are to find an increasing number of women in the same. One-third of all certified engineers are now women, and over three-fourths of all health workers at primary level are women. It is estimated that almost one-third of all certified medical researchers, banking employees, IT workers and chartered accountants are women. In a country bursting with an entrepreneurial spirit, today almost every fifth entrepreneur is a woman. With their increasing participation in a variety of fields, women's bargaining power in both private and public life is steadily increasing.

9. Insights from the Chapter

It is observed that women participation in work is more amongst poor and declines with family income and education. For example, in a study of over 100 countries, female labour force participation was found to the first decline with per capita incomes, and rise only when women became more educated and had access to high paid white-collar jobs.

It is suggested that to eradicate poverty at the grass-root level; the best way is to adopt Base of Pyramid (BoP) model, which aims to create job opportunity for the poor and marginalised people and involving them in socio-economic development. It is suggested to create employment opportunity through entrepreneurship. Creating entrepreneurial opportunities will help them to grow and eradicate poverty which will reduce the gender gap. Various studies have highlighted how lower female labour force participation or weak entrepreneurial activity drags down economic growth. Empowering women has significant economic benefits in addition to promoting gender equality.

Low female labour force participation rate (FLFPR) in India is declining when compared to any other region in the world . Demand-side or structural factors and supply-side or cultural factors like family roles and societal norms impact FWPR.

Another critical point of attention is that women still contribute a disproportionate amount of unpaid work in their homes and on farms.

Despite having more control over their finances, they are not given an equal say in household or work decisions.

In India, with the introduction of gender budget, resource allocation of the budget has contributed positively to prioritising women's role in different sectors. Studies have shown that with affirmative action and quotas for women for political representation; they can voice their opinion in a much more effective way. It has also increased the livelihood of women being engaged in the labour force. The participation of women in the workforce is influenced by the significant wage differential and forcing women to stay at home.

To support women and improve access to finance, numerous schemes have been introduced by the Government of India like Rashtriya Mahila Kosh, NABARD Schemes, etc. Other studies have suggested that microcredit is used for consumption and not for productive investment. This is also not supporting women to become more productive. There are many institutions for providing microcredit to women for starting some entrepreneurial activities to earn their livelihood. However, women use this money in nonproductivity activities. Access to credit for women for productive purposes can be enhanced by enabling collateralisation of loans with cash flow or equipment.

For making women more productive and involving them in some entrepreneurial activities, various policies had been suggested include changes in public investment in infrastructure, safer and better transport, sanitation and water; the efficiency of government spending in health, education and infrastructure to the extent they impact women's time allocation.

The educated unemployed women reported that the growth of jobs for women is low overall. However, the recent developments in the area of women empowerment are extremely encouraging. The participation of women in combat roles in the Army is also strongly under consideration. The Olympics, Commonwealth Games, and a number of international sporting events including cricket have seen outstanding performances by Indian women. Even India's successful launch of the Mangalyaan and the record-breaking 104 Nanosatellites launched into orbit onboard a single rocket had a team of women scientists behind them. The development of new avenues for women is new hope for women-led development and women empowerment.

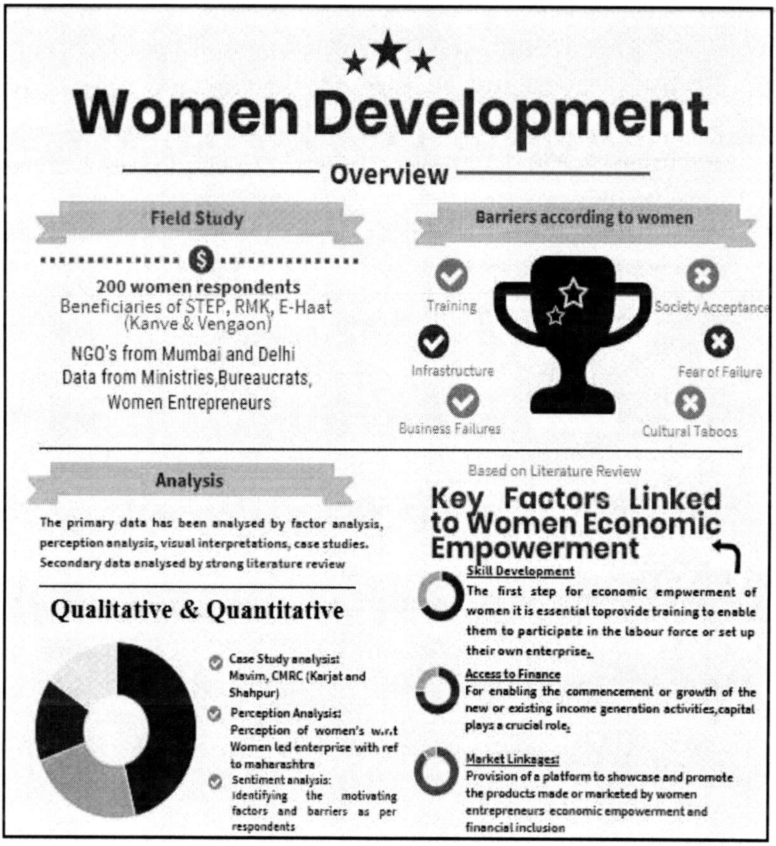
Women Development
Overview
Field Study
200 women respondents
Beneficiaries of STEP, RMK, E-Haat
(Kanve & Vengaon)
NGO's from Mumbai and Delhi
Data from Ministries,Bureaucrats,
Women Entrepreneurs
Barriers according to women
Training
Infrastructure
Business Failures
Society Acceptance
Fear of Failure
Cultural Taboos
Analysis
The primary data has been analysed by factor analysis, perception analysis, visual interpretations, case studies. Secondary data analysed by strong literature review
Qualitative & Quantitative
Case Study analysis: Mavim, CMRC (Karjat and Shahpur)
Perception Analysis: Perception of women's w.r.t Women led enterprise with ref to maharashtra
Sentiment analysis: Identifying the motivating factors and barriers as per respondents
Based on Literature Review
Key Factors Linked to Women Economic Empowerment
Skill Development
The first step for economic empwerment of women it is essential toprovide training to enable them to participate in the labour force or set up their own enterprise.
Access to Finance
For enabling the commencement or growth of the new or existing income generation activities,capital plays a crucial role.
Market Linkages:
Provision of a platform to showcase and promote the products made or marketed by women entrepreneurs economic empowerment and financial inclusion

Chapter - 5

Case Study of Mavim

The study is based on a combination of qualitative as well as quantitative approaches. The study was conducted to understand how SHGs are enabling changes in society with the help of Community Managed Resource Centre (CMRCs). Is also shows how CMRCs through the SHGs, are providing knowledge-based skill training and various activities that promote entrepreneurship. The research also studied the kind of training SHG members receive from CMRCs to promote social development and women empowerment.

The study includes two phases; the first phase identified the factors linked to women entrepreneurship and empowerment. The second phase focused on the views and perceptions of women entrepreneurs concerning barriers identified in women-led enterprises.

This exploratory and inductive study aimed to identify how early stage social businesses located in various centers might access finance to achieve growth. Because the study's objective was exploratory in nature, with a particular focus on the perceptions of women entrepreneurs, we developed a qualitative approach drawing primarily on focus groups to gather data. Subjectivism approach were adopted in this case because the social reality to understand various issues related to women are made from not only measurable indicators but also from the perceptions and consequent actions of social actors by use of language, conceptual categories, perceptions and consequent actions.

As we understand that group dynamics stimulate dialogue and allow a variety of views to emerge (Stewart *et al.*, 2007), therefore, the study had also conducted focus group discussions to stimulate dialogue. Focus groups which bring together participants from different perspectives may lead to informative discussions and can reveal unexpected findings that extend one person's opinion (Bedford and Burgess, 2001). In addition, focus group dialogues can show how opinions are formed and they provide an insight into social contexts as well as understanding about how stakeholders understand particular issues (McNeill and Chapman, 2005). All these aspects were relevant and important in this study. In order to address this issue, the focus group facilitators aimed to ensure that all participants could contribute equally revealing their opinions.

1. The objectives of the study

The study was conducted to understand the role of government schemes in encouraging women's employment and how women entrepreneurs and Self-Help Groups (SHG) facilitate changes in the social and economic upliftment of women.

The study was carried out with the following objectives:

- To evaluate the reach of three government schemes supported by ministry of 'Women and Child Welfare' - STEP, RMK and Mahila E-Haat in rural and urban regions.
- To study the qualitative impact of these initiatives on women beneficiaries, such as: an increase in confidence level, improved self-esteem, more participative approach, increased household decision making.
- To understand the limitations of these initiatives and give recommendations.

2. Mahila Arthik Vikas Mahamandal, Maharashtra (MAVIM)

The Shramshakti Report of the National Commission on Self-Employed Women and Women in the Informal Sector (1988) emphasizes on the need for a mediating body between the self-employed poor women and the financial institutions. This calls for the setting up of organisations like MAVIM as their focus is on working at the grassroot level for poor women. They are in a better position than banks to understand the characteristics of local markets and clients due to their intimate functioning with poor women. Such organisations can serve as important influences on the access of financial services to low-income group households. Improved access to savings can help reduce these households' exposure to external shocks and can also help to ease out their cash flows. (MAVIM)

MAVIM- The Women Economic Development Corporation, was founded on 25th February 1975 with the aim of encouraging women to be financially independent and self-reliant. Initially, it functioned through seven regional offices in Pune, Aurangabad, Nashik, Amravati, Nagpur, Thane and Mumbai.

MAVIM has been declared as a nodal agency by Government of Maharashtra on 20th January 2003 to implement various Women Empowerment Programmes through Self Help Groups (SHGs). The headquarters of MAVIM is in Mumbai. MAVIM has offices in every district of Maharashtra to implement developmental schemes for women in rural areas.

2.1 Initiatives of MAVIM for Women Empowerment

- **Entrepreneurship Training Programmes**

  MAVIM has 'Entrepreneurship Training Programmes' for livelihood opportunities available in the market. MAVIM also aims to impart education to women in sanitation, hygiene and nutrition. MAVIM is providing governance skills in women through leadership training programmes and Panchayat Raj Institutions (PRI) programmes giving information about the functioning of Panchayats. (Mavimindia)

- **Maharashtra Rural Credit Programme**

  The Maharashtra Rural Credit Programme (MRCP) is a poverty alleviation programme supported by the International Fund for Agricultural Development. MAVIM ensured that along with their economic development, the political and social developmental should also be addressed and a strong sense of 'self' was inculcated for making women self-sufficient and empowered.

- **Federation of Self-Help Groups**

  The idea of promoting SHG federations was suggested to the groups as a way of ensuring the sustainability and continuity of the SHGs. Federations promoted by MAVIM are designed as a two-tier model. Even after the time-bound programme like the MRCP came to a close in 2002, the groups constantly felt the need for guidance from the Sahayoginis.

  Though the savings groups had strengthened the economic aspect of their lives, the women felt that the dynamic support of the Sahayoginis was necessary to meet their other SHG developmental needs. Hence they were ready to contribute towards the part payment of the Sahayoginis' honorarium in return for receiving their services. In the initial stages, the members did not readily accept that all groups could not come together at the village level, nor did they agree to nominate an executive committee and have a federation at the cluster level. A series of meetings of all group members from the villages were consistently held at every district where the importance of each level of the federation was explained to the women.

To create a viable alternative to the role played by the Sahayoginis at the village level, it was decided to strengthen the groups and form a combined committee of all such groups at the village level to undertake the tasks of village development and other social activities. This, in turn, led to the efforts of creating a comprehensive, stronger unit at the cluster level in the form of a 'Federation'.

- The structure of the federation arises from the needs and motivation of the women, and the emergence of such a structure is a step towards the empowerment of women.
- Such structures primarily address training needs and of establishing forward linkages for the SHGs.
- A Federation of such self-help groups functions as informal, financial institutions. It is essential that their progress up to this stage be carefully monitored.
- In Maharashtra, SHG federations established through the old groups formed under the MRCP.
- The motivating agency is not a part of the management, especially the financial management of the SHG federation, to reduce the dependency on the motivating agency.
- MAVIM followed a two-tier model of SHG Federation.

(i) Village Level Committee (VLC)

All savings groups established in the village together formed one committee, with two representatives from each group. This committee had to facilitate the establishment and guidance of new savings groups in the village, take up village development activities, recommend deserving proposals of the group to the cluster federation, etc.

(ii) Cluster Level Federation (CLF)

The federation was formed from a maximum of 30 groups from 5 to 6 villages in a radius of 12 to 16 km. A maximum of 500 SHG members were allowed to make one federation. Each savings group member paid ₹ 30 per year towards the registration fees. These federations opened accounts in the bank, and the registration process of the federation was carried out. MAVIM is committed and is making efforts towards extending financial support to the savings groups through the federations. Such financial support could be from the various government and semigovernment financial institutions. Village Development Committees and Federations were established in the 12 districts where the MRCP was implemented.

MAVIM believes that the formation of the federation is the most important step in the developmental process of self-help groups. Irrespective of which scheme an SHG may have originated under, if it has to sustain on its own strength after a limited period of external support, then the formation of a federation is ideal. Over a period, it was realised by MAVIM that women members in the federations were unable to cope up with the growing volume of financial work and needed professional help for these transactions. On the lines of DHAN Foundation and MYRADA, MAVIM also started working on the concept of Community Managed Resource Center (CMRC), i.e. to promote people's institutions as a step further in the SHG movement. MAVIM promotes the CMRCs under the 'Tejaswini Maharashtra Rural Women Empowerment Programme' (Sangati, 2010).

Self-Help Groups (SHG)	Village Level Committee	Community Managed Resource Centre
• Social mobilisation • Financial Services • Organisation and Networking	• The link between SHGs and CMRC • Development of Village	• Programmes • Administrative control • Financial Planning and Control • HRM • Legal Structure

Before		After
• Lack of mobilization of savings • Limited access to credit • Lack of market awareness • Least scope for employment • No optimum use of skills and resources • Lack of confidence amongst women • Bounded by patriarchal system • Asset accumulation	**Post CMRC Intervention**	• Proper Financial Management • Easy access to credit • Improved market knowledge and access (E.g. Seed) • Capacity building • Increase in level of confidence (E.g. Construction of toilets) • Challenging the norms • In a position to make strategic life choices

3. Implementation of Various Schemes Supported by Central Government

In this study, three schemes were selected from the National Mission of Women Empowerment which is directly related to helping women empowerment by providing training for developing skills among women. The schemes chosen were: STEP scheme which promote training and development for women, E-haat for promoting marketing activities and Rashtriya Mahila Kosh for financial support. These three schemes have been selected with an objective to understand the concept of women empowerment through three different enabling factors:

(1) Capacity Building through training addressed by Support of Training and Employment Programme (STEP) scheme

(2) Provision of Access to finance through Rashtriya Mahila Kosh (RMK)

(3) An initiative of Mahila E-haat for access to market

STEP	Rashtriya Mahila Kosh	Mahila E-haat
The primary motive behind choosing this scheme for NMWE was that skill development related training forms a critical component in fostering sustainable and endured entrepreneurs as the latter is better equipped to deal with the business opportunities available.	Women lack physical/financial collateral to offer against loans provided by banks; in this context, RMK solves this problem as it gives finances from social collateral. Though funds are small but provide critical and foundational help in undertaking business activities by RMK beneficiaries. Hence this scheme has been finalised as one of the NMWE.	This scheme was chosen because women apart from salaried and regular paid wages jobs need to establish themselves as an entrepreneur. In this context E-Haat scheme has been one such scheme, which provides a platform for women to sell their products online with other E-commerce platforms.

All three projects aim to enhance the employability, financial ability and marketing understanding which will lead to the empowerment of women through entrepreneurship.

4. Support for Training and Employment Programme (STEP)

The Government of India recognises the need for a skilled workforce to meet the increasing demand for skilled human resources in the country. Thus, GOI has targeted an ambitious plan to train 500 million individuals by 2022, which on average translates into 42 million in a year. This calls for enhancing and upgrading the existing training infrastructure in order to meet the ever-increasing skilled workforce requirements of the country.

STEP being a 100% central government scheme has been in existence since 1986-87. Within the specific context of STEP, training is slated to provide to women who are poor and marginalised and training is being provided in traditional trades which mostly belong to informal sector. An important objective of STEP scheme is to provide sustainable livelihood generation through building and fostering traditional knowledge of women. A brief taxonomy of the STEP scheme has been provide through Table 5.1 as follows-

Under the STEP scheme trades covered consists of sector for imparting skills related to livelihood generation and entrepreneurship identified by the MSDE and includes the following trades:

- Agriculture
- Horticulture
- Food Processing
- Handlooms
- Traditional crafts like embroidery, Zari etc.
- Gems and Jewellery
- Travel & Tourism, Hospitality

Table 5.1: Taxonomy of STEP Scheme

Objective of the STEP Scheme	To provide skills that provides a sense of employability to the women To provide competencies and skills that enable women to become self-employed/entrepreneurs.
Target Groups	Under the STEP scheme, women's who are 16 years of above age can benefit under the scheme.
Eligible Organisations/ Project Implementation Agencies	Under this scheme organisations such as autonomous organisation under a specific statute or as a Society registered under the Societies Registration Act, 1860 or Indian Trusts Act, 1882 (Not for profit) or other statutes can work as implementing agencies. Voluntary Organisations or Non-Government Organisations registered under the Societies Registration Act, Indian Trust Act carrying out activities which promote the objectives of the STEP programme, with adequate financial and other resources, credibility and experience of the type of activities to be undertaken.

It is in the 7th five year plan that allocated INR 459 million for STEP programme under ministry of WCD and ministry of HRD. The scheme basically aimed at upgrading the skills of poor and asset-less women, mobilise them and provide them with the training and employment on sustainable basis in the sectors identified for them. One of the biggest benefits attached with the STEP scheme was that there was an inbuilt flexibility of project under the different sectors and each project suited to meet the local and sectoral needs. Under the scheme working capital for maintenance of productive assets is provided for supplementary activities leading to increased production. STEP as a training scheme has the potential to reach to the poorest of women through active intermediaries like NGOs and can reach to far flung areas of the country in larger numbers (Mishra, 1996). Goel (undated) argued that STEP is an assisted programme by central government that aims at employment cum income generation and the programme offers summarised courses of education and vocational training programme for women. The study by planning commission found that STEP's implementation at grass root level was weak at various levels and in many of the projects under STEP, linkages with the government departments and NGOs were not established. Below is the Table 5.2 which gives an account of number of beneficiaries under STEP scheme. One could gauge from the data provided in Table 5.5 that in 2017 number of beneficiaries under STEP scheme has decreased significantly (however for many states data is missing/unavailable) which might impede us in getting complete picture of performance under STEP programme.

Table 5.2: Selected State-wise Number of Beneficiaries Covered Under Support to Training and Employment Programme for Women (STEP)

Scheme in India (2014-15 to 2017)

States/UT	*Beneficiaries Covered*			
	2014-2015	*2015-2016*	*2016-2017*	*2017-2018**
Andhra Pradesh	800	2000	2191	-
Arunachal Pradesh	-	450	-	-
Assam	50	675	1600	-
Bihar	-	-	400	200
Chhattisgarh	-	-	400	200
Delhi	-	-	150	140
Gujarat	-	-	-	-
Haryana	-	-	200	-
Himachal Pradesh	-	-	-	-
Jammu and Kashmir	5500	-	200	200
Jharkhand	-	-	200	100
Karnataka	6666	6298	4434	-
Kerala	770	350	-	100
Madhya Pradesh	520	975	2014	300
Maharashtra	3609	125	350	180
Manipur	1505	2925	2250	450

(Contd...)

Meghalaya	-	-	-	-
Mizoram	-	-	-	
Nagaland	563	-	-	
Odisha	250	-	300	100
Punjab	5000	-	-	-
Rajasthan	250	-	200	-
Sikkim	-	-	-	-
Tamil Nadu	-	-	-	-
Tripura	-	-	-	-
Uttar Pradesh	1810	985	2850	2180
Uttarakhand	3180	-	500	50
West Bengal	480	-	-	-
India	30953	14783	18239	4200

Source: Indiastat.com.

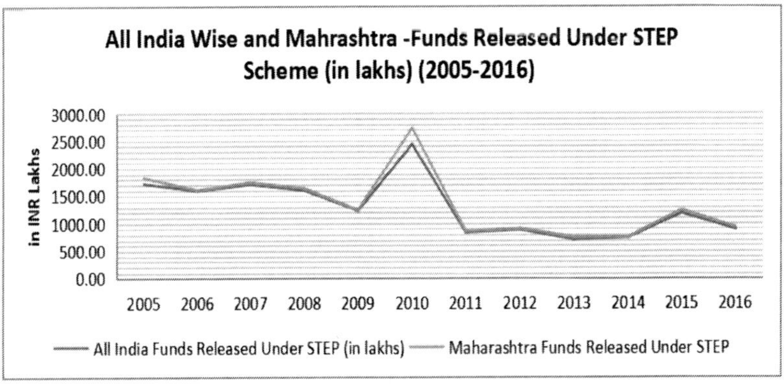

Figure 5.1: Fund Released Under STEP.

Talking specifically in context of women, to the best of available data on women related training under STEP, it could be inferred (see Table 5.4) that physical and financial achievements under STEP (number of beneficiaries and actual expenditures on scheme respectively) showed decline and from 2007 to 2012, both number of beneficiaries and financial targets has experienced under achievements respectively.

In this context, MWCD (Ministry of Women and Child Development) through its scheme titled Support for Training and Employment Programma (STEP), attempts to address some of the skilled workforce issues, especially concerning poor women in the far-flung areas of the country, where women may not be able to venture out beyond their immediate surroundings. STEP is a 100% central government scheme and has been in existence since 1998. The scheme provides training and employment for the holistic development of women. The purpose of the scheme is to give employability to women while also training for competency and skill, so as to encourage self-employment and thus women entrepreneurship.

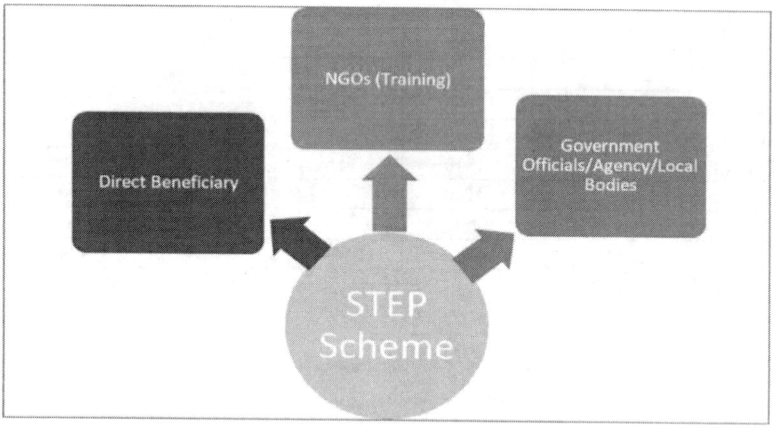

Figure 5.2: Stakeholders for STEP Scheme.

5. Rashtriya Mahila Kosh

This scheme was started by the ministry of WCD in 1993 as a national scheme to provide microcredit to women for their socio-economic empowerment. RMK acts as an autonomous body under the ministry of WCD and is registered under the Societies Registration Act 1860 (PIB July 2015). The operational model of RMK involves the aid of NGOs or facilitating agencies which are provided with funds that further on lend to

Objective of RMK

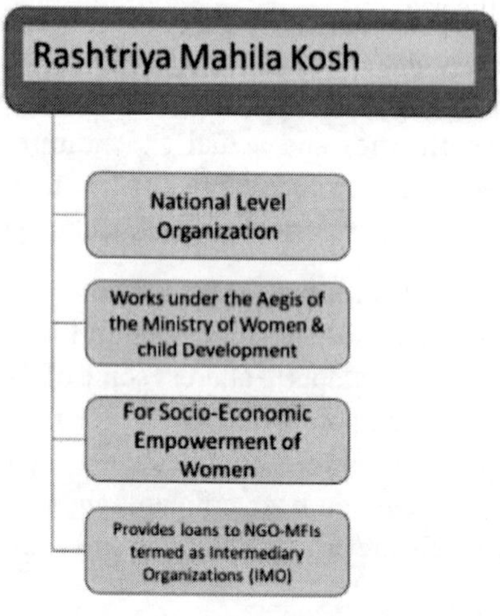

SHGs. RMK intends to provide microfinance to the weakest section of women; especially those sections that have fewer women entrepreneurs, who generate income taking help of loans from intermediary agencies at a low-interest rate of 6% who in turn can lend to SHG beneficiaries at 14% of the simple rate of interest.

The primary objectives of the RMK are to facilitate access to credit as an instrument or leverage for socio-economic change and development of women in totality. The RMK further aims to promote the schemes that provide employment opportunities directly and indirectly, the creation of physical as well as financial assets and to create and encourage entrepreneurial activities of women.

(i) Rationale for Choosing RMK

Finance occupies a critical element in fostering entrepreneurship as it provides the life-blood to carry out business activities. In this context, RMK based on solidarity principles and group/peer pressure attempts to finance mutual help groups formally called SHGs. Herein, finance is provided to the group and later on finance/loan is availed by individual members, but payment of the default of individual members lies with the whole group, thus implying lesser default and a more nuanced financial discipline. It has been often seen that women lack physical/financial collateral to offer against loans provided by banks. In this context, RMK attempts to solve this problem by providing finances from social collateral. Though finances are small, they provide critical and foundational help in undertaking business activities by RMK beneficiaries. Hence this scheme has been finalised as one scheme for projects under NMWE. Figure 5.3 provides a flow chart for RMK for the said project to explain stakeholders involved in RMK scheme.

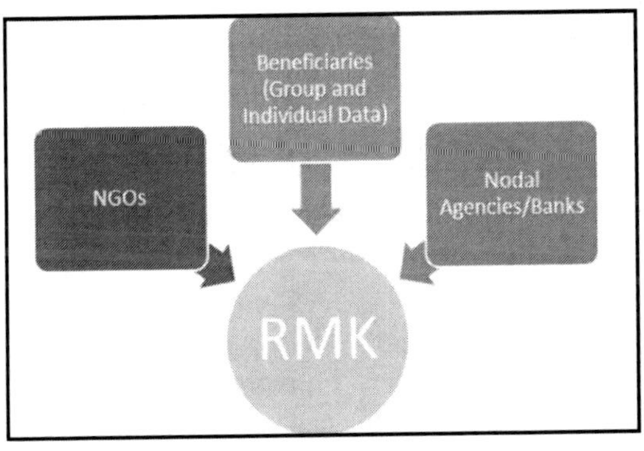

Figure 5.3: Stakeholders for RMK.

6. Mahila E-haat

With a view to promoting women entrepreneurship, Ministry of Women and Child Development (MWCD) came up with this innovative scheme in 2016, which attempts to bring to the fore entrepreneurial abilities of women in India. Additionally, it aims to meet the aspirations of the women as entrepreneurs with effective use of leveraging the technology for achieving the same (PIB March, 2016). This is a scheme that is a unique blend of technology and entrepreneurial abilities of women, which will uplift the socio-economic status of women in India. The scheme was addressed to those women entrepreneurs who run small businesses and are not able to access other online e-commerce. With this scheme, more than 10000 SHGs and more than lakh beneficiaries would be benefitted.

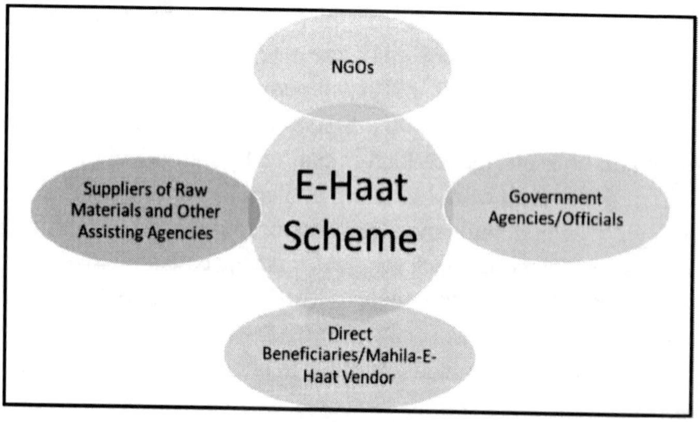

Figure 5.4: various Stakeholders of E-Haat.

Rationale for Choosing E-Haat Scheme under this Project

In the specific context, study is to broadly understand women entrepreneurship as a component of NMEW. This scheme was chosen because women, apart from salaried and regular paid wages jobs, need to establish themselves as entrepreneurs. In this context, the E-Haat scheme has been one such scheme which provides a platform to women to sell their products on the lines of other E-commerce platforms. Often women face supply and logistics related issues (including promotion and advertisement related issues) which hinders their capacity to scale up their businesses or even start new ones. Entrepreneurship leads to innovation, creativity and inculcates risk taking capacity into individuals.

Chapter - 6

Field Study

SECTION -I

A. Kayapalat CMRC, Kanave, Shahapur (Dist: Thane)

(i) Kayapalat at a Glance

Kayapalat CMRC focusing on livelihood mission has successfully targeted 35 number of villages in sharper. Forming 399 SHG and consisting of about 5415 members. In the financial year 2018, ₹ 12.32 cr credit has been given by the banks to the SHG members while MAVIM has maintained the repayment rate of 98% successfully in this financial year. The over all credit has been reached to ₹ 2.37 cr during the same year by the banks.

Shahapur is purposely selected for the study as it is one of the tehsil in the tribal zone under Thane District more than half of the population. It consists of 5415 members of the households of which 294 belong to the SC category and 1013 belong to the ST category. Out of 5415 members, 3616 belong to OBC category, and 269 members belong to minority category as per the report given by MAVIM personals.

Kayapalat CMRC is working with 35 villages in Thane district, which caters to around 5415 women. All CMRC functions are invigilated by the manager who is in charge of all the activities in the CMRC. (Government of India, 2011).

In the financial year 2017-18, ₹ 12.32 crore credit had been given by the banks to the SHG members. The accountant manages all these accounts related to loans and credit recoveries. While focusing on the livelihood mission, CMRC has successfully targeted 35 villages in Shahapur by forming 399 SHGs. The reason behind selecting Shahapur for the study is that it is one of the tehsils under Thane District, where more than half of the population belongs to the tribal community. (Government of India, 2011)

The status of a number of members of the SHGs formed under the programme with the breakup of categorisation of members is given in the following table.

Table - 6.1

Sl. No.	*Name of the category*	*Total number of SHG member*
1.	SC	294
2.	ST	1013
3.	OBC	3616
4.	Minority	269
5.	Others	223
	Total	**5414**

MAVIM focuses more upon livelihoods which resulted most of the women MLP are part of "KUKUT PALAN" which helped them to develop an innovative idea of building a community cadre of "KUKUT PALAN". The objective of the cadre is to provide handholding support to MLPs in terms of regular meetings of MLP members, follow up vaccination cycle by members, introducing new practices such as rearing of the small chicken (PILLU) to a fully grown chicken. Overall 240 women have been trained in 2018, these chicks are purchased at ₹ 1 from the other bachat ghat and

Field Picture 6.1: Researchers with Bachat Ghat group at KAYAPALAT CMRC.

later they are rared into half grown chicken these are then purchased from the other group who grows them and the fully grown chicken are then send to the nearby markets. Other focused areas under MLP (Micro-livelihoods Plan) are dairy development, backyard poultry, vegetable cultivation.

(ii) About Kanave

Kanave is a Village in Shahapur Taluka in Thane District of the Maharashtra State, India. It belongs to the Konkan region and Konkan Division, having a total population of 872 which consists of 428 women (49.1 %) and 444 men. The total literacy rate is 68.7% (599) out of the total population, in which the female literacy rate is 28.4%. (Government of India, 2011).

KANAVE village is selected for the present study. Members of SELF HELP GROUP were selected as sample for the study, two of the three women representing their bachat ghat where selected by the Shayoginies. 30 members were selected from 20 SHGs. SHG members belonging to various social-status were surveyed. Only females members belonging to different age group both from tribal and nontribal communities were surveyed. One CMRC office from every above-mentioned group was selected for an interview. Assistant District coordinating officer supported the research team to get involved with them for the interview purpose at CMRC.

A descriptive study of 45 female respondents was conducted. Many respondents were illiterate whereas the remaining respondents have a low educational level which made them difficult to write and understand the questionnaire. Based on our field study, focused group discussion, and personal interview, it is clear that the working of the SHG, CMRC, and MAVIM requires lots of cordination and system and process to involve women for working in a group and promoted them for various activities for their development. The study in Kanave village was conducted during September 2018. The information was collected through a well designed and well tested questionnaire.

(1) Age Group

The responded was classified into four age groups such as Table 6.2.

Age Group (In Years)	*Number of Members*	*Percentage of Members*
16 to 25	1	1.3%
26 to 35	16	35.6%
35 to 45	17	37.6%
46 to 70	11	24.6%
Total	45	100%

The table indicated that the highest percentage of members is 37.6 % belonging to the age group of 35-45 year. which shows that the female participation in the SHG are experienced and are of middle age group. The reason of involvment of these group was basically these women wants to repay the loan or get the loan. Another reason was as per our inquiry was they want to change their life style and bring the change in eating and living pattern. 24.5% belonging to 46-70 years which is the most senior and experienced members. Whereas only 2 % of members consists of young and energetic.

(2) Education

The information about education was obtained from the interview which is as follows:

Table - 6.3

Education	*Number of Members*	*Percentage of Members*
Illiterate	23	51.1%
Primary	10	22.3%
Secondary	6	13.4%
HSC	5	12%
College Level	1	2%
Total	45	100%

As per the data it is obserevd that more than 50% of women working in SHG are illiterate. During our interview process it was clear that although they are illiterate but they have enough excitement and motivation for working in group of women for improving the quality of life. The result shows that there is much more need to improve the educational level among the SHG members to improve the efficiency level which will lead to improving the developmental conditions of the members. Although 22% have received primary education, but only 1% among the rest is graduate.

(3) Primary Occupation

For understanding the source of income of the women it was necessary to understand their occupation which is as follows:

Table 6.4

Primary occupation	*Number of members*	*Percentage of members*
Agriculture labour	11	22.3%
Agriculture allied activity	19	44.4%
Other	15	33.3%
Total	45	100%

The data indicates that 44.4% of the women are engaged in agricultural activities like vegetable cultivation, allied activities like selling of milk in their areas. The vegetables are also sold in the wholesale markets like Bhiwandi and APMC market in Vashi apart from their own marketplace.

Whereas 33.3% of the women are engaged in other activities like tailoring and beautician. Only 22% of the women are labour doing the field work for cultivating crops.

(4) Training Programme

CMRC provides training facilities to their SHG members, funded by the MAVIM. The training is provided for improving skills, gaining knowledge and empowering women socially and economically. The aim of the CMRC is to upgrade the women within their bachat ghat through various training programmes.

(i) **Women livelihood program** – Through this programme women are taught about how women can change there current economic and social condition by understanding there inbuilt talent and most importantly their self-existence in self can bring changes in their life.

(ii) **Capacity building** – where they are trained to build in self-confidence and ability to work in the outer world which leads to the upliftment of women in the society and reduce the gender gap. They also provide training such as English speaking classes, internet classes, learning about Android technology (how to use touchscreen phones), bank related and market knowledge to make them self-empowered.

(iii) **Agricultural activities** – The women use primitive and traditional methods for cultivating crops which consume more time, resulting in low productive level and affecting the health of the women severely, looking to this issue CMRC has provided an "Agricultural toolkit" (this toolkit is available in the village) which consists of all the modern equipment and machinery such as tractors, harvesting machine, diesel pumps, thresher machine, sprayers, brush cutter. These equipment are provided to the group of SHG members those who are part of backward linkage programme on loan to convert them into the forward linkage program. That is necessary and required for cultivation, these women are trained and timely updated about the recent tool used for agricultural activities thus increasing the production level and spending lesser time in the field, along with this the women have trained the easier methods for rice husking and cleaning them.

(iv) **Micro livelihood plan-** CMRC is implementing micro livelihood programme at the grass root level, it has 20-30 women SHG members where they are involved in implementing MLP in a group. The group members of the SHG can be a part of different SHG group where they come together to form one MLP group.10% of the amount is brought by the SHG members, 20% comes of the project that they involved in to create assets. These assets are not given as fund but as a revolving fund, and the remaining 60% is through bank linkage programme.

(v) **Dairy Activities** Besides agriculture dairy activity is one of the most important livelihood options for rural people. To increase the production of the milk SHG members cultivate Mazzola, hydroponic grass and green fodder. The intervention of the CMRC helped the women to increase the quality of the milk and also helped them to sell their dairy products in the nearby markets. CMRC provides regular training for purchasing of pesticides, seeds to retailers. They also trained women involved in, by imparting knowledge about the seeds, pesticides, insecticides which are suitable for the particular crop.

(vi) **Backward linkage programme -** Lack of market knowledge and awareness about the market, women's paid more for the seeds and for the fertilizers creating a group of backward linkage programme. The Shayoginies along with the SHG members were given practical training about the market knowledge, creating awareness about the price structure.

(5) Financial Linkages

(i) SHG and Bank Linkage Programme

Under this programme, banks provide loans to these SHG members at 2% every month making it annually repayable at 24%, to the SHG members for various purposes such as an educational loan, agricultural loan, marriage loan and business loan. These loans are lent from the banks on bases of the activity processed by the SHG group. Once the loan is repaid to the banks, then the banks give the fees to the CMRC at 1% The SHG members for various purposes such as an educational loan, agricultural loan, marriage loan and business loan.

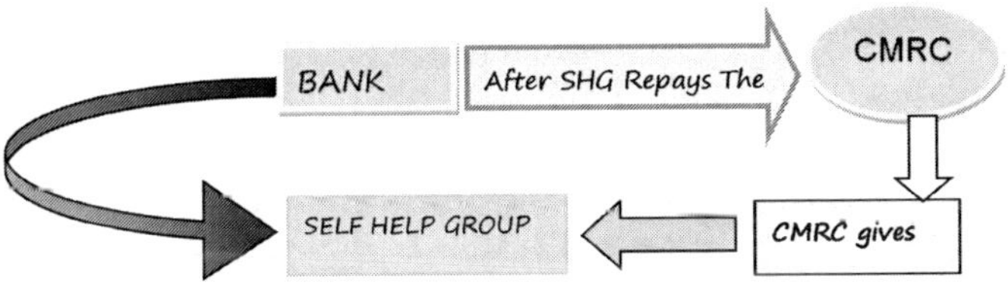

Figure- 6.1

(ii) Micro-finance

The ICICI and IDBI bank grant loans to the CMRC at 1 % interest to the SHG. 148 SHG members received 66658 amount of loan during the year 2017-2018, although they had a target of ₹ 2.91cr which is yet to be achieved. CMS with the bank linkage programme provides LIC policies to the SHG members at 1% interest rate, bank participates by sending their agents on the field to ensure that maximum SHG members have policies with them.

The 1% is also used by the CMRCs for providing loan for gricultural activity, agro service center, hartivahan, mother unit, Agro tool bank, trading activity pashu khadya.

(iii) Enterprise developmental activities

CMRCs provide enterprise development activities in agriculture service center like training them to use the aggro tool, new methods for cultivating, giving them proper knowledge about the pesticides, unaware women used different chemicals for different crops it leads to decrease in production, market knowledge about the market pricing of the seeds. Lack of market knowledge forced the women to pay the extra price for the seeds. Agriculture is one of the major sources of the livelihood of the people it was necessary to provide training to the women as they spend more time on the field cultivating crops.

After the training provided by the CMRC the women of the village feel more confidence in performing agricultural activities like (crops, horticulture, livestock, vegetable, spice, cattle feed, and pastry) which enhances their livelihood support, besides non-farm activities helps to increase their potential and demand of group members. (e.g. beauty parlor training, pashu palan training, technology training, embroidery training, mobile training etc). Training is provided to develop market linkage and is taught about marketing by giving practically training to the SHG members and setting up the market for the women where they can supply their products and their products are outsourced at a wider range.

Picture 6.2: Meeting With Women Entrepreneurs

Picture 6.3: Research Scholars from VESIM With CMRCs Team During Month of October 2018.

Based on our field study, focused group discussion, and personal interviews, it is clear that the workings of the SHG, CMRC, and MAVIM require multi level coordination, following various systems and processes involving women for working in a group and promoting multiple activities for their development.

B. Pragati Community Managed Resource Centre, Vengaon, Karjat

1. Demographic features

Vengaon is a village located in Karjat Taluka of Raigad district in Maharashtra. The sex-ratio of Vengaon village is around 944 compared to 929 which is average of Maharashtra state. The literacy rate of Vengaon village is 69.05% out of which 71.3% males are literate, and 66.67% females are literate. There are 1.43% Scheduled Caste (SC) and 4.29% Scheduled Tribe (ST) of the total population in Vengaon village.

1.1 Occupation

The primary occupation of the people in Vengaon is fishery. During the offseason, people undertake cultivation of vegetables and engage in animal husbandry. The Pragati CMRC covers 44 villages having 212 groups consisting of approximately 2000 women.

1.2 Structure of the Pragati –CMRC

The Karjat taluka belongs to the rural areas, so there was a need to develop an Urban Livelihood Block (ULB) at an urban level too. At present, there are four ULB undertaken by the testing programme, i.e. Khopoli, Navi Mumbai, Thane, and Karjat.

The Tejaswini programme has benefitted around 6034 SHG members from all the blocks as mentioned earlier. And at Karjat, there are 2789 SHG members where a livelihood officer is in charge of the SHG groups.

The number of personnel at CMRC is 26, which consists of 5 area coordinators, 6 Sahayoginis, 4 staff members, 11 other members who are involved in Marketing, Advertising, maintaining the accounts, bank linkage programme, keeping track of records, etc.

1.3 Activities of SHGs under Pragati CMRC

The CMRC provides training for jobs like beauticians, embroidery/tailoring, agriculture training, selling vegetables and goat rearing. During their slag season, the women were trained with the rearing goats as their alternative work to earn for their living.

From the tailoring training given to the SHG women, these women have started manufacturing and selling cloth bags in the wholesale market. Besides, the CMRC also gave an opportunity one such group member to run a stall in Alibaug which is a picnic stop; these women have put stalls and sell their *garam masala* to the tourists.

1.4 Demographic Profile of SHG respondents in Vengaon Region

The case study was conducted to understand the whole of Vengaon region to give a complete picture of the improvement in the status of women through SHGs. Out of 30 SHG groups, 21 were present for the interview, and they represented their own respective SHG group. The information was collected through a questionnaire; the 1st classification was on age, caste, and their occupation.

Table 6.5: Classification of Respondents Based on Age Group

Age Group (in years)	*Number of members*	*Percentage of members*
20 to 30	04	19.5%
31 to 40	09	42.85%
41 to 50	05	23.8%
51 to 60	03	14.2%

(i) Age Classification

Table 6.5 indicates that the highest number of SHG members belong to age group 31 to 40, which indicates that 42.85% of the women belong to the middle age group. This shows that these women were targeted by the **Sahayoginis (Sahayoginis were appointed by CMRC to mobilize the women to get them involved in the SHG).** The focus of Sahayoginis was to target women who were engaged in domestic and unproductive chores. A lesser number of respondents belonged to the age group between 51-60. This is due to their higher age, because of which they could not actively participate in the SHG activities. However, they can help solve the problems that other members face.

(ii) Education of SHG Members

As per our survey 47% of the members have completed their primary education and 38% were reported as they are illiterate. This also indicates that lack of financial sufficiency forces them to drop their schooling. SHG members help them by training them to read and sign. The main aim of the SHG members is to promote savings and get credit for the productive activity. It is important to give different training to SHG womens like financial training which be helpfull for them to understand the workings of the bank and other facilities related to credit and loan.

Table 6.6: Classification Based on Education Levels

Education	*Number of Members*	*Percentage of Members*
Illiterate	08	38%
Primary	10	47%
Secondary	03	15%
HSc	00	0
College Level	00	0
Total	21	100%

(i) Primary occupation

Table 6.7: Classification based on Primary Occupation

Primary occupation	*Number of members*	*Percentage of members*
Agriculture labour	01	04.79%
Agriculture allied activity	18	85.71%
Other	02	9.5%
Total	21	100%

Income is the major component of the standard of living of the people. The revenue of the SHGs have increased after they joined the training sessions, as 85.71% of them are now engaged in agriculture allied activities making it their primary occupation, like selling of agricultural produce (vegetables and dairy products). As their earnings increase, their purchasing power helps them to understand the market mechanism; slowly and gradually they are capable of taking personal loans from the SHG group and turning into entrepreneurs in their respective areas.

C. Ghe Bharari CMRC, Chembur, Kurla

1. About Chembur

Chembur is one of the largest suburbs in eastern Mumbai, India. Chembur comes under Ward M East. Its Area is 32.5 km^2 with Population: 8,06,433 (as per 2011 census). According to the ward wise census analysis, 236 it was observed that M East ward, which comprises Chembur, Deonar, Anushakti nagar, Govandi, Trombay and Mankhurd, has the highest slum populations in the city, with 72.5% of its population living in slums. It's in this ward that large colonies of the poor have been resettled since the 1970s to make way for industrial expansion and later for projects like Mumbai Urban Transport Project.

1.2 Demographic Profile

(i) Age group

Table 6.8: Demographic Profile

Age Group (in years)	*Number of members*	*Percentage of members*
20 to 30	05	12.5%
31 to 40	20	50%
41 to 50	10	25%
51 to 60	05	12.5%
Total	40	100%

The above table shows that 50% of the women belong to the middle age group who joined SHG. After interviewing them, it was clear that at this age they feel more responsible because suddenly, expenses increases in the family due to the growing age of their children and expenses of education etc. All these matters motivate them or for some time compel them to work for the family to maintain the quality of life.

(ii) Education

Education plays an essential role in decision making, working efficiently, earning more and getting a better position in the group. During our interaction and systematic study, it was found that the proportion of literate women in the urban area is more than the rural area due to awareness among family members to educate the female members of their family. Being educated makes a difference in their lives, and it helps them make fast decisions, earn more and saves them from exploitation.

Table 6.9: Education Level of SHG Women at Kurla CMRC

Education	*Number of Members*	*Percentage of Members*
Secondary School	26	65%
HSc	10	25%
College Level	04	10%
Total	40	100%

(iii) Occupation

Table 6.10: Occupation Level of SHG Women at Kurla CMRC

Occupation	*Number of Members*	*Percentage of Members*
Sale of Handmade Products	05	13%
Housewife	05	13%
Skill Training	10	24%
Cooking	15	37%
Parlour	5	13%
Total	40	100%

Other than SHG formations, various kinds of courses are also conducted by MAVIM for example, courses on making multiple products such as agarbatti, phenyl, washing powder, liquid soap, chocolate, cake, snacks, flowers, and jams. In addition to these, MAVIM also conducts courses for jobs such as beauticians, computer training and tailoring etc. Health camps are also organised to provide free checkups and make women aware of the vaccinations etc.

Survey conducted show that 13% of the women were involved in selling products such as art and craft items, bags, etc. as compared to 13% of those who prefer to stay at home. 24% of women are assigned to provide skill training to uplift them from difficult conditions. To upliftment these women, CMRC conducts training programs in the fields of culinary training and parlour training to provide them with home-based employment. Thus these women get involved in snacks making and take orders during festive seasons and provide tiffin services to the working class family.

SECTION - II

Field Data Analysis and Interpretation

1. Support for Training and Employment Programme (STEP)

The researcher selected 75 women representatives, as they belonged to the SHG. The women beneficiaries undergo various training programmes that encourage their self-reliance and autonomy by enhancing their productivity and enabling them to take up income generating activities, in different sectors like-

- Agriculture and nonagricultural activity like animal husbandry.
- Tailoring and Embroidery.
- Fisheries and dairy.
- Food processing like making chiwada, chatnis, and snacks.

The government conducts training programmes for rearing animals and creating alternative work like selling dairy products like milk and curd in their village markets which includes 20% of the women involved along with fisheries. 25% of the women are engaged in tailoring and stitching, embroidery related work as it is convenient for the women beneficiaries as they are provided with the material and infrastructure, besides women get an opportunity to work from home as they do not have to travel much. 13% of the women beneficiaries are engaged in the food processing business.

1.1 Micro Livelihood Plan- (MLP)

Through these programmes, women are trained on how they can change their current economic and social condition by understanding their inbuilt talent and most importantly their self-existence in self can bring changes in their lives.

1.2 Agricultural and allied activities

The women use primitive and traditional methods for cultivating crops which consume more time, resulting in low productivity and efficiency simultaneously harming the health of women. Therefore, these training programmes include sessions on maximising the agricultural yield by using modern techniques where CMRC established an "Agro Tool Bank" which is located in the village. It consists of all the modern equipment and machinery such as tractors, harvesting machine, diesel pumps, thresher machine, sprayers, brush cutter.

Micro Livelihood Programme (MLP) focuses on creating livelihoods at the grassroots level. CMRCs have a significant role in implementing Micro-Livelihood Program (MLP) at the grass root level where agricultural activities like vegetable cultivation; other allied activities like dairy and poultry farming were considered.

Through MLP, women gain sufficient knowledge on improving dairy production by using techniques covered in sessions.

CMRC provides regular training on purchasing of agricultural inputs such as pesticides, seeds and fertilisers, etc. from merchants. They also impart knowledge about the proper usage of seeds, pesticides, insecticides which are suitable for the particular crop.

Under MLP, poultry farming model has proven to be successful which has helped in building a community cadre of poultry farming. The objective of the cadre is to provide support to members belonging to MLP in terms of regular meetings, following up through Sahayoginis, introducing new practices in poultry farming from rearing of the small chicken to a fully grown chicken. Overall 240 women have been trained under this during 2016-17.

Initially, due to the lack of market knowledge and awareness, women paid more for the seeds and fertilisers. But through CMRC intervention, the SHG members underwent practical training about the market knowledge where the awareness was created on purchasing agricultural inputs at the right price.

1.3 Livelihood and Women Empowerment

Along with the above, the programme also focused upon Social Enterprise Activities by CMRCs. Social entrepreneurship is the recognition of a social problem and uses entrepreneurial principles to organise, create and manage a social venture to achieve a desired social change. While a business entrepreneur typically measures performance in profit and return, a social entrepreneur also measures positive returns to society. Thus, the main aim of social entrepreneurship is to broaden social, cultural and environmental goals.

Maturity for these activities takes 3 to 4 months, as this has started in the current financial year. The finances for these activities project funds but restrict them to 20-40% depending on the gradation of the CMRC.

66% of the Social Enterprise activities fall in 3 key types, i.e. Agro Service Centers, Goatary related activities like Goat Bank/ Buck unit/ Breed Improvement centres etc. & Cattle Feed Selling/Manufacturing. The other activities under social trading of pulses, poultry, cashew unit, garment units & banks etc. programmes under Social enterprise activity are E-catering under Indian Railway Catering & Tourism Corporation (IRCTC), Vocational Training Programme centres (VTPs) registered under Maharashtra Skill Development Society (MSDS).

MAVIM has done many innovative partnerships like IRCTC-e-catering, Internet Saathi (Google India-Tata Trust project)- Internet access to the rural area, Aakar Innovations –to provide affordable, high-quality sanitary napkins, ICICI Foundation –supply of Aprons to training institute, UNDP-tie up with marketing.

1.4 Impact of Training

It was recorded that post training programme, women were empowered by conducting a business activity which helps them increase their monthly income. Around 50% of the women contribute in their household income by paying electricity bills, buying durable items like mixture, cooker, gas stove, mobile phones etc. and durable items. 15% of the women help in repaying their husband loans or repay their loan that they have taken for personal use for marriage and educational purpose.

Around 70% of the women did not face any restrictions from the family, but these womens expressed their views that initially (45%) they experienced restriction from their family members as family members were unaware about the training program which they were going through. These women also shared their views that family members believed that they would forget their responsibility towards their families.

Nearly 5% of the women beneficiaries viewed that despite being aware of their work these womens were restricted because their family members had a conventional mindset, and these members were thinking that women are violating the social norms of breaking the patriarchal system and their dependence on their family member would decrease.

45% of the women have started with their own business after they received training, training helped women beneficiaries in various ways like they enhanced their skills, received professional training for producing quality goods. These women received training like renting space for their shops, selecting the place where they can gain profit, providing materials and so on.

Continuous capacity building training played an essential role in empowering women. Nearly 85% of the women were engaged in agriculture and allied activities. Also, though 38% of the women were illiterate, they did not assume literacy level as an obstacle in improving the quality of life.

All the representatives expressed their views that they have noticed a change in their behaviour and their personality, they believed that undergoing training has helped them in increasing their confidence level, have become more knowledgeable about the current market. These respondent have shared that they started understanding themselves more than they did before, they can fight for their rights, understand what is right and wrong for them, developed a feeling of bringing change in their society.

CMRC training programme facilitates women in improving skills, gaining knowledge and empowering women socially and economically. With the support of CMRC women were able to establish their social business where these women were able to support their families as well as for community also.

MAVIM funds these programmes with the aim to upgrade the skills of women and promote community led development in the villages. By various schems programmes, women are given training to gain self-confidence which provides them with the ability to work in a competitive environment leading to their upliftment. Training is provided on basic communication skills, financial literacy, existing market knowledge and trends and sessions on basic utility of mobile phones to keep themselves updated.

1.5 Collaborative Efforts

Ghe-Bharari CMRC has successfully created a market linkage programme with retail chain Big Bazaar for supplying spice powders and various Chatnis. Until 2017, the members of the SHG were successful in delivering more than 100 kgs of Masala and Chatnis.In 2018, Ghe-Bharari inaugurated food van which is managed by SHG members.

2. Rashtriya Mahila Kosh (RMK)

2.1. Microfinance Services

The Tejaswini programme: The inception of the Tejaswini programme, MAVIM has taken initiatives for providing financial services through SHGs as credit finance is being a crucial factor for the economic development of SHGs/Members. The programme put efforts upon savings and social security to SHGs. Hence the primary focus of the programme listed as follows:

- Generation of savings amongst SHGs
- Access to bank loans to SHGs
- Social Security to SHGs through insurance and pension services

The researcher interviewed 75 women representation from the SHG groups.

Where 70% of the women expressed that they did not face any problem for registering themselves as a member of RMK as they are part of the SHG groups. 5% of women revealed that they had to face issues as they did not have proper documents of their identity.

The researchers found that 70% of the women belonged to scheduled caste. These women feel that being part of SHG has helped them to change their social and economic status. Since they are earning a source of their family members, so they are getting more importance in the family. These women are treated as idol in their village inspiring the younger generations of their village, they viewed that undergoing through various training such as like chiwda making, snacks making etc. and financial literacy programme like LIC policy for women and children, different life insurance schemes like children's education has helped them to increase their knowledge and improve the economic conditions of their family members.

35% of the beneficiaries preferred granting loan within their SHG loan. Despite having a good earning income of ₹ 25000-30000 because they could help the other women in setting up business as these beneficiaries are answerable to their NGO and were not forced to mortgage any ornament which the bank demanded and they received maturity period of 3 years at times for 4 years depending upon the reason of loan granted. This has helped women to produce goods and earn income, and the low-interest rates helped them to repay the loans.

2.2 SHG and Bank Linkage Programme

CMRC spreads awareness among SHG women various schemes related to the bank through financial literacy. The SHG members receive loans from private banks like ICICI and Bank of India. The SHG women found the procedural hindrances in acquiring loans from the public sector banks owing to the tedious process and endless paperwork. This was perceived as a discouraging factor by women as it was time-consuming.

Under this programme, banks provide loans to SHG members at 2% every month making it annually repayable at 24% interest from ICICI and IDBI bank. Generally, the loan is taken for consumption or productive purposes. Funding for domestic necessities such as children's education, marriage, medical or any other emergencies come under consumption loans. The loans that are used to establish, renew or upgrade an existing business are considered to be utilised for productive purposes.

Once the loan is repaid to the banks, then the banks give the 1% as service fees to the CMRC.

The total amount of bank loan received by SHG members in the year 2017-18 is ₹ 2.37 crore. CMRCs with the bank linkage program also provides LIC policies to the SHG members through field correspondents to ensure that maximum SHG members have policies with them to mitigate unforeseen risks.

2.3 Purpose of Loans and Ownership of Assets

The members of the SHG required credit for the following purposes: General Household Expenses, Marriage of Daughter, Repair of House, children's education, Medical Expenses, and husband's occupation.

Since loans could be for more than one purpose, the purpose with most considerable amount has been taken as the main reason for borrowing. It was observed that the loans for the general household expenses were availed by those members who had borrowed more than once from the groups. It was encouraging to find that the most significant number of women had acquired to start or support an income generating activity. This indicates that these women and their supporting groups were moving on to the diversified use of the loans. The overall income levels being rather low for the majority of women it was not surprising that the loans for general household expenses were necessary for the women. These women were also found to be very concerned about the education of their children. While the loans for the tuition of school going children figured prominently in education-related loans in very few cases, it was also used for payment of fees for various courses. These were the contingencies which the households have to face frequently.

3. Mahila E-haat

3.1 Eligibility Criteria for registration on E-Haat

The eligibility criteria of the women are that they should be of 18 years of age. While registering for E-Haat they need to be a part of the SHG group for at least 3 years irrespective their age and their records as a member of the SHG group. The NGO or the SHG group should have their brand if not then they should develop their brand along with the E-haat logo and should be part of the SHG programme or should be associated with NGO to display their products on E-haat.

This study shows that it took 2-3 week maximum for the women to become part of the E-haat and 20% of the women felt it took more than 6 months to join the E-haat schemes and these women had to follow a process of submitting document step to become part of the E-haat schemes.

3.2 Contribution to the Household Income

Researchers observed that all the members of E-haat were earning women and contributed to the household activity and their revenue increased from ₹ 10,000 -15,000 per month after they become part of the E-haat. The NGO with whom they were associated provided them with infrastructure facilities for producing goods along with the raw material.

3.3 Impact of E-Haat on Women Beneficiaries

MAVIM has also tied up with "Mahila E-Haat" an initiative by Govt. of India to showcase SHG products. In the WESE vertical, the focus was upon male sensitisation to create enabling environment, develop the system to follow up and track social activities, Gender focal person, create enabling environment for the gender of staff along with family members, provide legal support to the SHG members.

The researcher observed that 50% of the women gained their confidence level as they had expanded their business on the online platform. And they learned to travel to different places for conducting exhibitions and selling their products adding to this the representative viewed that after their monthly income increased their family supported them and allowed them to travel to different places for training and selling purposes. 45% of the women feel that have improved their standard of living after being a part of the E-haat because they could buy good quality of food, educate their children and could buy non-durable goods as well.

18% of the representative feels E-haat has successfully helped them cover broader market and wish to connect people globally as their products are getting good response and feedback besides they can repay their loan along with contributions in their household expenditure.

3.4 Social Empowerment Indicators

66% of the women can move to nearby areas, and in another state for conducting exhibitions and promoting their products. They did not have any restrictions because the NGO took care of their travelling expenditure, and in return these women earned double income. Increased income helped them to buy durable products, their savings increased. These women also able to acquire loan quickly which was very difficult in the past as they were neglected. These women beneficiaries were empowered to decide on purchasing any commodities as they earn.

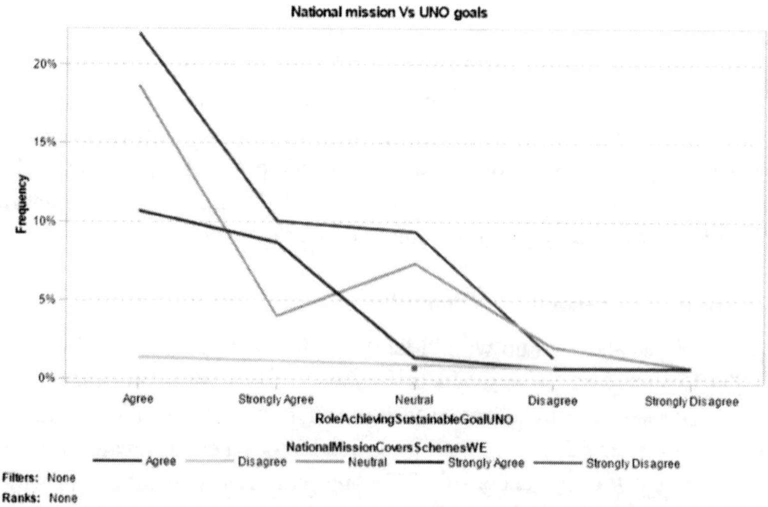

Figure 6.2: Trend analysis- National Mission & UN SDG Awareness.

Thus, with such kind of assistance and arrangement to seek confidence and enhance the abilities of the women's schemes are designed for the all round development of the economy by making a freeway for women entrepreneurs.

The study investigated the roles of women in achieving UN Sustainable Development Goals and its awareness, as well as the accessibility to a variety of schemes for women empowerment covered National Mission for Empowerment of Women of 2012. This dimension was crucial because awareness of projects and programmes at the national and international level will assist women in making informed decisions while and after establishing an enterprise.

Out of the total sample, 75.34% of respondents are aware of the UN goals. Figure 4 indicates the analysis that 79.34% of people agree about women having a definite role in achieving Sustainable Development Goal of UN and were also aware of the various schemes covered in National Mission of Women Empowerment.

4. Reflections from the Field

Reflections from the field collate certain observations of the researchers in understanding the enabling role of SHGs that have subtly given a social space to marginalised women in raising their voice and negotiating with the status quo for better decision-making within the household.

SHG members during their meetings, strongly reflect upon their concerns for issues such as alcoholism, benefits of alternative energy sources for daily cooking, matters related to childcare and maternal health and wellbeing. In some cases, women have been able to resist incidents of domestic violence at the hands of their alcoholic husbands. Similarly, women in groups have raised their voice with the administration for providing the facility of potable water in their village, use of forest products as fuel, which saves their time about the collection of fuel and water. SHGs can be conceptualised as **"communities for women"** that provide social identity to all its members. This framework allows women to acquire the preliminary social abilities of negotiation and decision-making while they are engaged in community-level actions. They often transgress their household boundaries and engage in collective activities such as alcohol banning, indigenous seed saving practice, organising campaigns for maternal health and safe immunisation, and marketing homemade products. These activities, which reinforce a sense of "the self' can be individual or collective self among women; thus, empowerment begins in a contextualised manner.

Thus, in the field areas, SHGs have become an organised space to offer solidarity and collective identity to marginalised rural women and provided the possibility of credit at the doorsteps. On the contrary, field data also reveal an increasing burden on women to repay the loans that they have drawn through micro-finance institutions. In this sense, we can infer that gains in women's economic status and their entitlements may be symbolic or limited in nature due to the prevailing patriarchal attitudes within the household.

Based on our field study, focused group discussion, and personal interview, it is clear that the working of the SHG, CMRC, and MAVIM requires lots of coordination and system and process to involve women for working in a group and promote them for various activities for their development.

SECTION - III

Perception Analysis of Women Concerning their Understanding of Women-Led Enterprises

Data was also collected to understand the perspective of the sample of 120 female respondents from across various regions of Maharashtra which includes Karjat, Shahapur, and Mumbai. Primary data was collected from women respondents from each region who were connected to either entrepreneurship, linked with any government scheme, part of an SHG, CMRC or who have a direct or indirect connection with empowerment, enterprises, or business. Another objective of primary data was to understand the role of government schemes in rural and urban areas in facilitating empowerment of women. Probability sampling technique is used for this study, which includes stratified sampling and snowball sampling. Layered sampling technique was carried out in which the researcher targeted the sample of respondents primarily available, who were following the above mentioned criteria, i.e., women running a business or either way connected to entrepreneurship, and they were initially focused in the first phase of data collection. Later, snowball sampling technique was used to collect the data for this study. References from the primary respondents were obtained and using this referral, and further interviews were carried out from the sample of respondents based on similar characteristics and criteria.

In this section of the study the perception on different aspects related to entrepreneurs, empowerment and livelihood matters has been identified during survey interview process.

1. Awareness

1.1 Awareness of UN sustainable goals and National mission schemes for women enterprise: Women and girls, everywhere, must have equal rights and opportunity, and be able to live free of violence and discrimination. Women's equality and empowerment are one of the 17 Sustainable Development Goals, but also integral to all dimensions of inclusive and sustainable development.

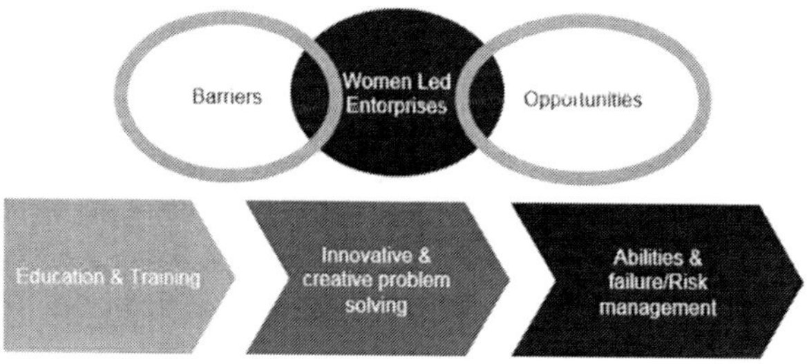

Figure 6.3: Representation of Data Analysis.

Goal 5 states that:

> End all forms of discrimination,violence against all women and girls in public and private spheres. Eliminate all harmful practices, Ensure women's full and active participation and equal opportunities for leadership at all levels of decision making against the women and equal rights to economic resources, as well as access to ownership and control over land and other forms of property, financial services, inheritance, and natural resources to all women and girls everywhere.

The sustainable development goals seek to bring positive change by addressing key challenges such as poverty, inequality, and violence against women. The study also aims to outline the critical targets of the standalone goal on gender equality and women empowerment by linking it to the national mission of women empowerment schemes for all round benefit of women.

Achieving gender equality and women empowerment is integral to each of the 17 goals. Only by ensuring the rights of women and girls across all the targets will we get to justice and inclusion, economies that work for all, and sustaining our shared environment now and for future generations. Promote the use of modern technology, especially in the field of information and communication, to enhance women empowerment. Through the use of computers and the internet, women can interact and learn from their counterparts in developed nations.

E-Haat motivates and encourages the women entrepreneurs with help and support of direct online marketing platform.

Table 6.11

UN SDG Goals Awareness	*National Mission Awareness*	*Responses*
Agree	Agree	79.34%
Disagree	Disagree	3.35%

The above table (Table 6.11) Indicates the Frequency of responses from target respondents who are aware of their role in UNO Goals and also aware of the National mission schemes. 79.34% of the respondents affirmed their awareness about both, i.e. UNO Goals and NMWE Schemes and only a small proportion, i.e. 3.35% Respondents disagreed in terms of responses.

Which states that the women had a clear understanding and awareness about their roles and responsibilities and also the knowledge about the national mission schemes which were existing for their self-development as well as achieving goals.

2. Perception Analysis

The Study further focuses on analyzing the perception of women over specific parameters which are linked to women entrepreneurship. This perception analysis helps in making the inference about the factors affecting women entrepreneurship which includes the following:

More emphasis is needed on women-led enterprises in rural and poor areas to understand the perception of women's comparing urban and rural conditions.

Girl's students in higher education colleges should be trained for taking up the projects to analyse their viewpoint with regards to more top education projects and training to emphasise women-led enterprises.

Women led enterprises to promote innovations in products and process factor was considered to understand the thought process of women about changes and practice w.r.t. women led enterprise.

Women entrepreneurs can compete on equal terms with men. It was observed from the literature that competence is one of the critical factors which also signifies confidence and to examine their outlook while comparing with men.

Similarly, various other factors such as professionally qualified women can promote sound enterprises. It is feasible to train potential women Entrepreneurs, Women in urban area can compete for more than in rural areas, Leadership qualities like perseverance are more visible in women entrepreneurs, Society still does not accept women as a source of potential entrepreneurs. Women, in general, have better abilities to negotiate and solve problems. Women entrepreneurs tend to be more creative because of different challenges, most social enterprises led by women in India have a professional background.

Women led enterprises have also excellent opportunities for business diversification. In long term Women have definite role in achieving sustainable development Goal. The national mission for women of 2012 covers a variety of schemes for women empowerment, and to achieve national mission cross cultural training is required to develop women entrepreneurs. Women led projects can contribute to digital economy. Social enterprises with higher involvement may produce beneficial results for stakeholders, counselling facilities and arrangements for women entrepreneurs in modern business. The perception of women over various 265 parameters such as training, education, difference of perspective, involvement and contribution, opportunities, barriers etc. and its linkage in women Entrepreneurship were included in analysis.

2.1 Competency

The study concentrated on the perception of women across Maharashtra. These findings about competencies had a significant impact while summing up various other depending factors. Therefore, it was essential to know about the perception with respect to competencies and whether there exists any gender bias in this factor.

Past research has mainly concentrated on the role of leadership in large corporations, ignoring the small enterprise context (Vecchio, 2003). Similarly, despite the literature attributing female entrepreneurs' "different" attitudes on areas such as leadership, profit, and growth (Marlow and McAdam, 2013; Sexton and Bowman-Upton, 1990), little research has particularly focused on females as an explicit research group (De Bruin, Brush, and Welter 2007).

Finally, with respect to competencies, in line with past studies, the female leaders in this study perceived themselves to be well equipped with entrepreneurial and personal competencies, but not so much with managerial skills (Heilbrunn, 2004). They indeed seem to highly trust their communication, human relations, and interpersonal skills as well as their ability to be creative and take advantage of opportunities, but not their administrative, marketing, sales, and financial skills. What particularly interesting is that most of our respondents are not highly educated or with rich experience in related or non-related industries, and not with great support from their immediate-close environment.

Whereas, the weaknesses or lack of prominence in leadership roles were associated with barriers, such as lack of education, family, and workplace restraints or gender-related discrimination. Thus we studied

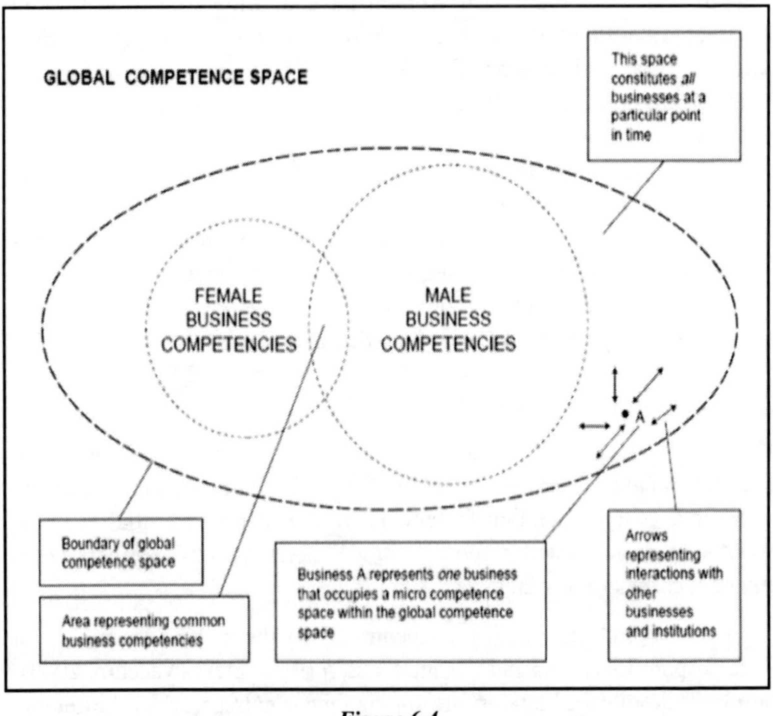

Figure 6.4

about their perception when it comes to competence relating to entrepreneurship.

Research and practice related to competence are motivated by aspirations to achieve superior performance, acknowledging the increasing interest in female entrepreneurship and the role of women in the global economic environment in the current study, we also focus on the role of competencies in shaping the leaders.

2.2 Correlation: The drivers of General Enterprise v/s Women-Led Enterprise

While studying about the women's perception, w.r.t. women led enterprise another essential factor which carried weight was their viewpoint about the driving force of the enterprise. The determinants considered were social, institutional and government support and the motivation to run an enterprise.

Thus, the study was undertaken to analyse their understanding and perception about the driving force, the comparison and correlation between the drivers of general or male-led enterprise and women led enterprise.

As per the analysis of this study, out of the total population, 48% of the total sample agrees and reflects positively on the point that the drivers for women-led enterprise hold the same importance as that of general entrepreneurship.

Whereas 32% of the respondents have neutral perception w.r.t driving force for women-led enterprise and general enterprise and 20% of the respondents perceive that the driving factors for women-led enterprise and public enterprise are diverse.

2.3 Problem-solving abilities & Negotiation skills

Entrepreneurs encounter with several various challenges while setting up an enterprise. The problems are more especially in the case of a women entrepreneur as there are several social and external environment constraints.

Table 6.12

Negotiation Abilities	*Frequency*
Agree	64
Strongly Agree	60
Neutral	25
Disagree	1
Strongly Disagree	Nil

Thus, to counter the trials, an entrepreneur, in general, requires problem-solving abilities and negotiation skills at the place. To understand the perception of women when it comes to their abilities to solve problems and challenges concerning establishing enterprise, the frequency of sample on their acceptance and understanding about women's problem-solving skills and negotiating skills in comparison to men was analyzed.

One hundred twenty-four respondents out of total sample, i.e. 82.66% of the respondents agree with the statement that women's, in general, have better abilities to negotiate & solve problems and 25 respondents, i.e. 16.66% were neutral and only one respondent, i.e. 0.68% disagreed about their better problem-solving skills and negotiation skills. The perception of abilities holds strong acceptance that when it comes to women-led enterprises women can solve the problems and challenges in a better way.

2.4 Projects in Higher Education for Women led enterprise

Concerning this study, the perception of women's in context to available training for women entrepreneurship and the need for projects in higher education was analysed.

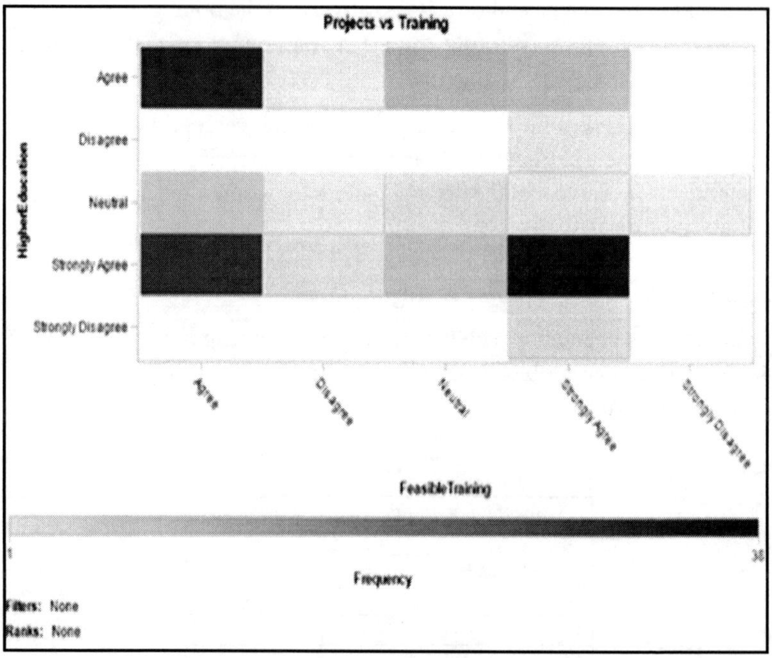

Figure 6.5

The above correlation matrix shows a strong association that it is feasible to train potential women entrepreneurs and projects should be taken while in higher education. Around 72% of the sample admits that it is feasible to train women entrepreneurs and it would be impactful if training projects would be included in higher education.

2.5 Opportunities through Microfinance

Various micro-finance schemes and other institutional support schemes have been initiated to promote women entrepreneurship. The impact of it has spurred women entrepreneur-ship but not to an expected level. Therefore, it was essential to understand the perception of women whether this support creates opportunities for women-led enterprises or not.

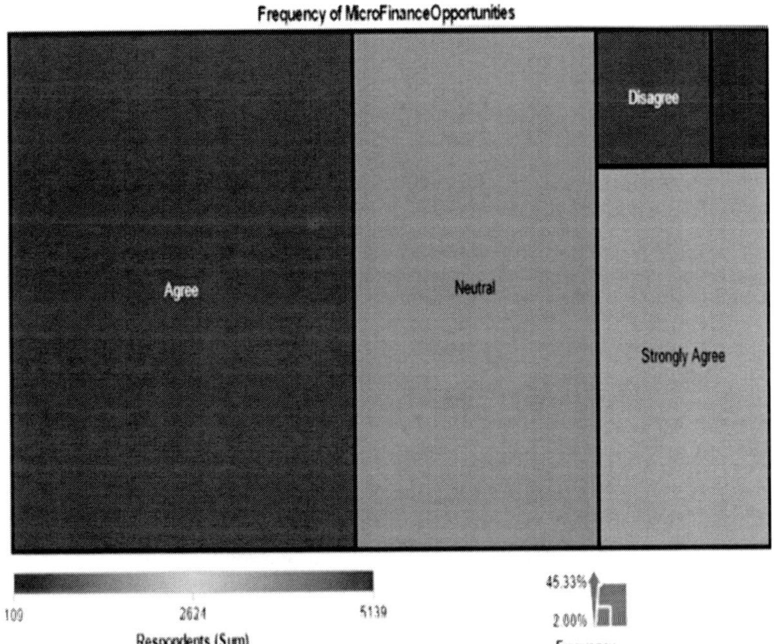

Figure 6.6: Tree Map – Micro finance opportunities.

Figure 6 presents the result that 62% of respondents agree on the fact that microfinance creates opportunities for women-led enterprise whereas 6.35% of respondents disagree that such support does not generate opportunities for women-led enterprise.

2.6 Emphasis on Training

The trend line represents the perception analysis of the respondents over their viewpoint while comparing the urban and rural scenarios when talking about women entrepreneurship and emphasis on training.

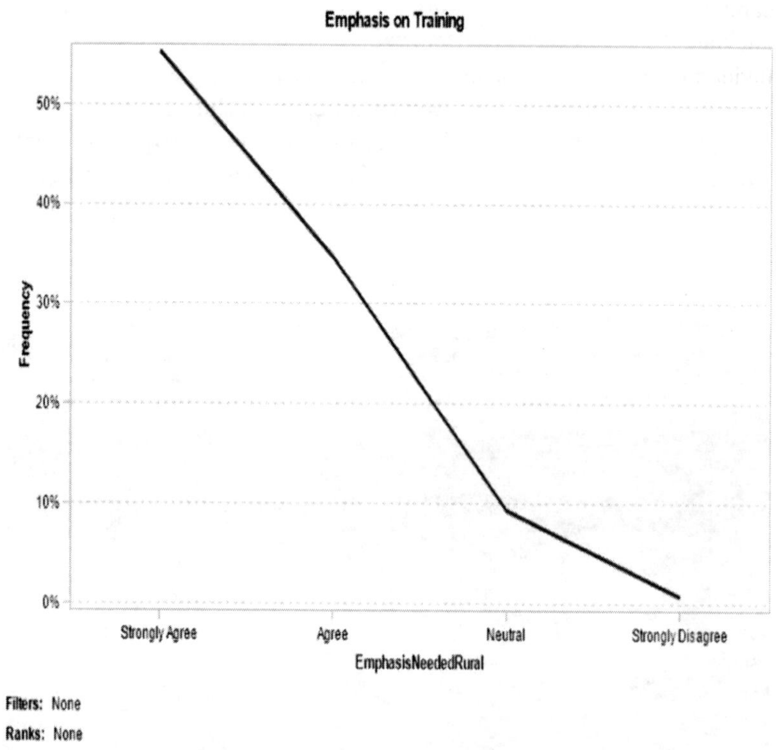

Figure 6.7: Trend- Emphasis on training.

Figure 6.7 indicates that 55% of the respondents hold the perception that more emphasis is needed in rural and poor areas for women-led enterprises. They agree that gap exists in training facilities provided to women in rural and urban areas.

2.7 Financial Interventions

Out of the total 120 women respondents, most of them had a minimal amount of initial investment the below present visual bar chart signifies the initial investment involved by women for setting up the enterprise. 40% of the women used less than ₹ 1 lakh (INR) of the amount, 21.6% of women required ₹ 1-5 Lakhs of initial investment, and 8.33% of women needed the amount between ₹ 5-10 lakhs.

Despite the existence of several schemes and programme for women; there exists a lack of awareness of projects for women enterprises. Thus, there is an urgent need to spread the knowledge of thc application through campaigns. An appropriate approach on the part of bank officials can alleviate the issues faced by women entrepreneurs for accessing finance under a particular scheme.

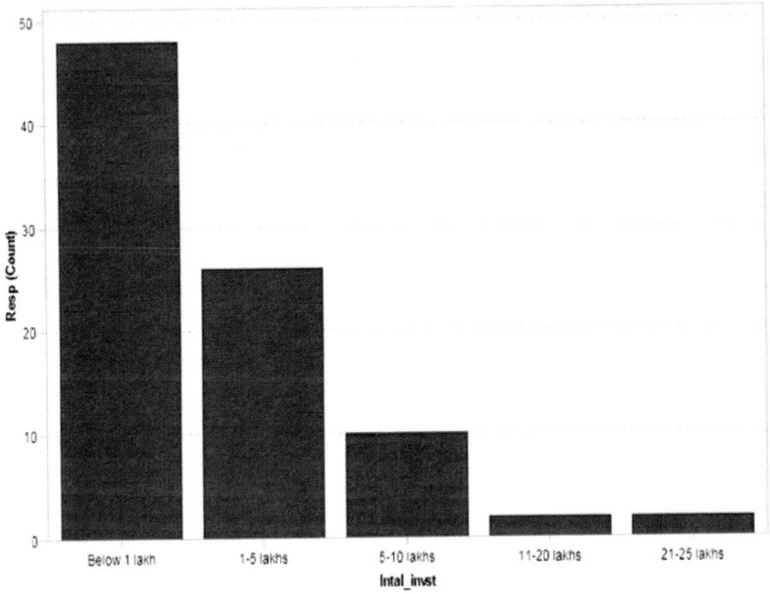

Figure 6.8: Financial Interventions.

2.8 Impact of education and projects in higher education for entrepreneurship

Entrepreneurship education offers women's such opportunity by helping them anticipate and respond to change. Women's learn that (1) although a job may be accomplished today by performing a given set of tasks, tomorrow an entirely different set of functions (and skills) may be required; and (2) because businesses are always changing, workers need to find new ways to do given jobs or new ways to do a given job better.

It also promotes brainstorming of potential businesses in the various vocational areas as a means of making girls aware of self-employment as another route to success and personal esteem.

The level of women's empowerment and entrepreneurship increases positively with education. A higher proportion of women who are exposed to school or any projects have high confidence, are comparatively more innovative. Thus, the literacy status of the women's also has a significant impact on empowerment and entrepreneurship.

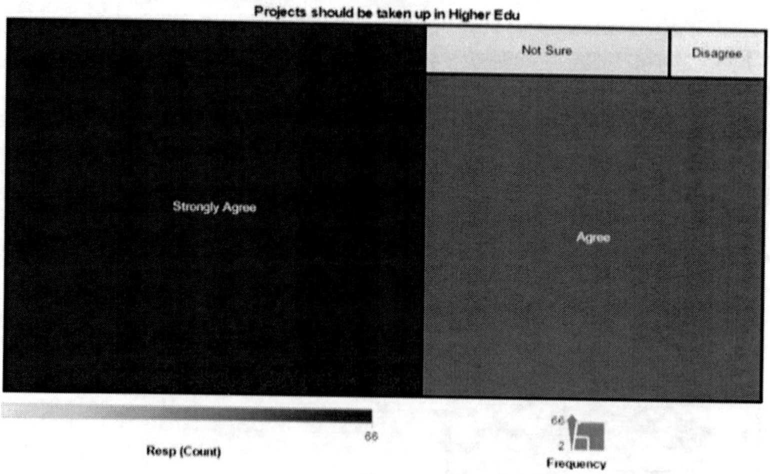

Figure 6.9

- The training module should be updated periodically to meet industry demands.
- The system should be designed to gauge and provide need-based training. Evaluation of competencies, inclination, and prior knowledge can be done to create the training programmes.
- The concept of entrepreneurship should be imbibed into girls at the school level which will help them in building entrepreneurial acumen. (Shah, 2013)
- As per the above analysis, this situation calls for collaboration between social enterprises, foundations, government commissions and agencies, consultants and the media. Working with the media to increase awareness of the concept, educate the public about which will be beneficial on a micro and a macro level.

2.9 Correlation Matrix: Negotiation Abilities vs. Business Failure Management

SAS Visual analytics studio was used to obtain the following correlation matrix over general variables, i.e. negotiation abilities and Business failure management.

As many as 49% of respondents expressed their affirmative that women, in general, have better abilities to negotiate and solve problems, as well as simultaneously disagrees women entrepreneurs may not be able to handle failures on a long term basis.

3. Factor Analysis

The study uses Factor analysis technique for analysing the patterns of complex, multi-dimensional relationships between the variables identified for women empowerment and entrepreneurship which defines and explains the identification of underlying model and summarise it into a small set of the factor.

Eigen Value is the latent root which denotes the amount of variance accounted for by the factor, Eigenvalue greater than 1 decides the number of factors.

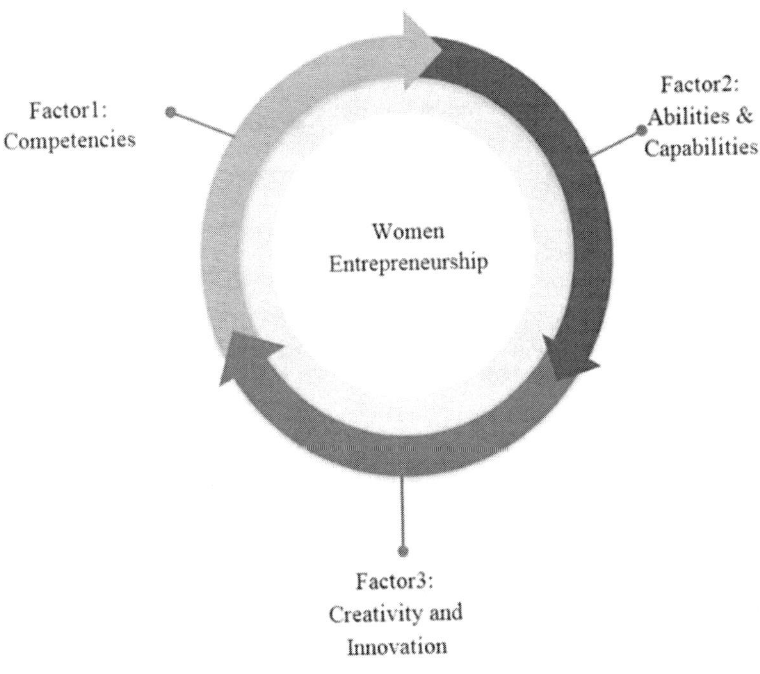

Figure 6.10

A measure of sampling adequacy is the measure calculated for both the entire correlation matrix and each variable evaluating the appropriateness of applying factor analysis, i.e. values above 0.50 for either matrix or an individual variable indicate suitability.

The Eigenvalue for three matrices is greater than 1; therefore, three factors will be retained as per criteria.

Factor Analysis Results

The FACTOR Procedure
Initial Factor Method: Principal Components

Eigenvalues of the Correlation Matrix: Total = 9 Average = 1				
	Eigenvalue	Difference	Proportion	Cumulative
1	3.21752258	1.89738967	0.3575	0.3575
2	1.32013291	0.20347691	0.1467	0.5042
3	1.11665600	0.28136695	0.1241	0.6283
4	0.83528905	0.08411391	0.0928	0.7211
5	0.75117514	0.17650743	0.0835	0.8045
6	0.57466772	0.14313570	0.0639	0.8684
7	0.43153202	0.00881449	0.0479	0.9163
8	0.42271753	0.09241046	0.0470	0.9633
9	0.33030706		0.0367	1.0000

3 factors will be retained by the MINEIGEN criterion.

Kaiser's Measure of Sampling Adequacy: Overall MSA = 0.75509984					
socity_WE	Abilts_slve prob	Girl_highredu	Womn_ownbuiss_a	WLE_invtn	Profly_chnlngs
0.81399123	0.70700209	0.75782359	0.60803834	0.80207514	0.78032172

Kaiser's Measure of Sampling Adequacy: Overall MSA = 0.75509984		
WE_cretve	Buiss_failar	Buiss_suprt
0.41152761	0.81131991	0.84672890

Prior Communality Estimates: ONE

3.1 Factors

Factor 1: Competencies for Women Entrepreneurship: Factor competencies briefly talk about the qualities and capabilities which should be comprised in the women entrepreneurship. Potential women entrepreneur should come up with innovative ideas and promote innovation in products and process while establishing women led enterprise.

Factor 2: Abilities: Women, in general, have better abilities to negotiate and solve problems as they go through many day to day challenges, they come up with various helpful alternatives which help them address critical issues in the easiest possible way. It is also understood that women shall come forward to start their own business instead of living in financial crises by utilising all the abilities and problem-solving skills.

Factor 3: Creativity: It has also been studied by understanding the perception of women w.r.t. women entrepreneurship that women entrepreneur tend to be more creative because of different challenges which they face in day to day life.

Pearson Correlation Coefficients, N = 120

Prob > |r| under H0: Rho=0

	socity_WE	Abilts_slve prob	Girl_highredu	Womn_ownbuiss_a	WLE_invtn	Profly_chnlngs	WE_cretve	Buiss_suprt	Buiss_failar
socity_WE	1	0.2831	0.44683	0.2355	0.45373	0.48636	-0.07944	0.30716	0.38151
		0.0017	<.0001	0.0096	<.0001	<.0001	0.3884	0.0006	<.0001
Abilts_slv	0.2831	1	0.16343	0.34394	0.28769	0.16576	-0.0605	0.11179	0.09522
	0.0017		0.0745	0.0001	0.0014	0.0704	0.5116	0.2241	0.3009
Girl_high	0.44683	0.16343	1	0.18713	0.23488	0.37187	-0.08083	0.13877	0.37595
	<.0001	0.0745		0.0407	0.0098	<.0001	0.3802	0.1306	<.0001
Womn_ov	0.2355	0.34394	0.18713	1	0.22982	0.13131	0.30307	0.16744	0.1849
	0.0096	0.0001	0.0407		0.0116	0.1528	0.0008	0.0676	0.0432
WLE_invt	0.45373	0.28769	0.23488	0.22982	1	0.49847	0.05223	0.23584	0.33047
	<.0001	0.0014	0.0098	0.0116		<.0001	0.571	0.0095	0.0002
Profly_ch	0.48636	0.16576	0.37187	0.13131	0.49847	1	0.10148	0.3421	0.54542
	<.0001	0.0704	<.0001	0.1528	<.0001		0.2701	0.0001	<.0001
WE_cretv	-0.07944	-0.0605	-0.08083	0.30307	0.05223	0.10148	1	0.12592	0.1982
	0.3884	0.5116	0.3802	0.0008	0.571	0.2701		0.1706	0.03
Buiss_sup	0.30716	0.11179	0.13877	0.16744	0.23584	0.3421	0.12592	1	0.43068
	0.0006	0.2241	0.1306	0.0676	0.0095	0.0001	0.1706		<.0001
Buiss_fail	0.38151	0.09522	0.37595	0.1849	0.33047	0.54542	0.1982	0.43068	1
	<.0001	0.3009	<.0001	0.0432	0.0002	<.0001	0.03	<.0001	

3.2 Barriers linked to women entrepreneurship

Word cloud is a great way to analyse underlying obstacles that most of the women entrepreneurs responded when they were asked for the restrictions related to Women led enterprise.

Despite having a positive perception of several factors such as abilities, skills, competencies, opportunities, there is the existence of constraints and barriers faced by women in an enterprise.

Table 13: Barriers linked to women entrepreneurship

Barriers	*Responses*	*Barriers*	*Responses*
Access to finance	16.81%	Shortage of funds and resources	7.56%
Education and Technical Training	15.13%	Lack of Market Experience	8.40%
Fear of Failure	15.13%	Lack of confidence	5.88%
Infrastructure	7.56%	Society acceptance	5.04%
Training	9.24%		

- **Social institutions and inequality:** In India, the cultural obstacle for women's participation primarily comes through the patriarchal system which is often against women's economic freedom. Religious attitudes determine women's financial involvement. Additionally, it also influenced by social class. In traditional societies risks of exposure to other males outside of the home has reduced female participation. Thus, self-employment within the house may be a way to overcome these social risks while raising participation in the labour force.
- **Infrastructure as an economic barrier:** Infrastructure such as roads, technology, access to water and electricity, safety and availability are few factors which can be positively used to enhance women participation. These factors also contribute to bolstering women entrepreneurship.
- **Education reduces socioeconomic barriers:** Knowledge is also one of the strongest determinants of female entrepreneurship in India (Daymard & Sorsa, 2015) because it assists them in building human capital, the required skills, and experience.

  Education brings several benefits to women where they are in the position to make decisions on their own and take advantage of economic opportunities. Education has complex socioeconomic linkages related to female well-being. Girls' access to education is influenced by marriage age, which in some parts of India is low.

  Over the years, much progress has been made to enhance the school enrolment of girls at the primary level. Nevertheless, more efforts have to made to further the reach of the girls to take quality secondary and higher education. A high unemployment rate is observed in more top educated women due to skill mismatch issues.

The bias between male and female begins at an early age in very subtle ways, and it is crucial to solve new paths of inequality that is more difficult and costly to resolve over time.

In India, many laws have been formulated to protect women's rights and guarantee for equal treatment.

- **Entrepreneurship policies:** The active training programmes have led to an increase in the number of female entrepreneurs in the manufacturing and services industry. Additionally, female entrepreneurship can also be facilitated by promoting role models and networks.

  Networks and agglomeration bring positive location externalities as a dense network of production and market opportunities can boost productivity and lower unit costs (Fujita *et al.,* 1999; Ghani et al., 2012) unless overtaken by congestion costs.

- **Access to finance:** Women with access to pension and savings in bank accounts are more capable of making independent decisions on resource use. Enhancing women's control over the resources increases their bargaining power in households (Duflo, 2012). There is also a strong relationship between women's financial inclusion and their performance as entrepreneurs in developing countries (OECD, 2012). Financial inclusion is considered as an essential tool to lessen poverty by promoting entrepreneurship, the creation of jobs.

  To improve access to finance for women, numerous schemes have been introduced, Rashtriya Mahila Kosh, NABARD Schemes, etc. Many studies have suggested that microcredit is used for consumption and not for productive investment. Access to credit for women for productive purposes can be enhanced by measures enabling collateralisation of loans with cash flow or equipment. Discriminatory loan practices whereby men sign women's documents in banks should be eliminated in law.

- **Equality of laws and economic opportunities:** In several countries, the government accountability on gender is limited, and often there is a lack of awareness about public services and the capacity to assess the impact of the policy of men and women. The agencies which work for gender equality have a low profile, and thus availability of gender-disaggregated data can be an issue.

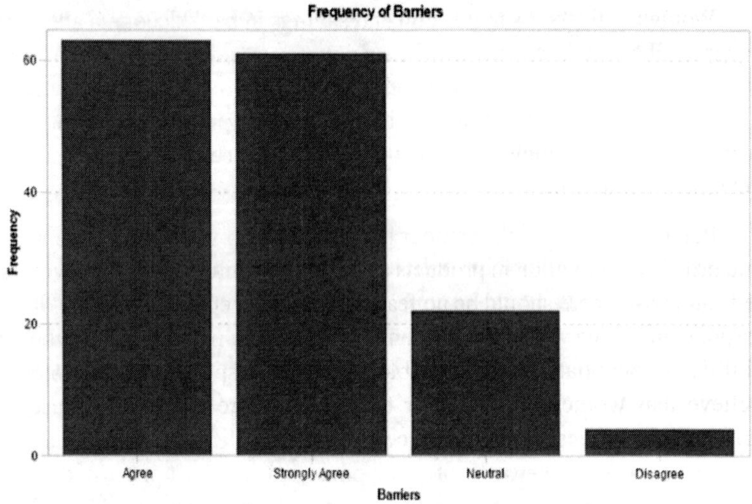

Filters: None
Ranks: None

Figure 6.11: Bar Chart- frequency of fear of barriers.

Figure 6.11 indicates that still, 82.66% of respondents agree that barriers in entrepreneurship restrict them from entering and surviving in entrepreneurship as there are many barriers to women entrepreneurship in general.

The study also emphasises the further analysis in identifications of barriers and eradicating or reducing it when focusing on women-led enterprise and women empowerment.

Key Learning

In the study it is clearly observed that the female leaders perceived themselves as well equipped with entrepreneurial and personal competencies, but not so much with managerial skills. They trust their community, human relations, and interpersonal skills. Women were found very confident for their creativity, they always wish to explore opportunities and take advantage of opportunities, but they felt that if they get some support for administrative, marketing, sales, and financial skills, they can do much better. Hence, the government, NGOs and other governing bodies should propose and implement these missing skills which are required by women. The training should be demand driven not supply driven.

Women with access to pension and savings in bank accounts are more capable of making independent decisions on resource use. Enhancing women's control over the resources increases their bargaining power in households (Duflo, 2012). There is also a strong relationship between women's financial inclusion and their performance as entrepreneurs in developing countries.

Potential women entrepreneur should come up with innovative ideas and promote innovation in products and process while establishing women led enterprise, there should be no fear of society acceptance. 82.66% of the respondents agree with the statement that women's, in general, have better abilities to negotiate & solve problems and 25 respondents, i.e. 16.66% believe that women entrepreneur tend to be more creative because of different challenges which they face in day to day life.

Chapter -7

Role of Women in Social Entrepreneurship

After independence of India, the constitution makers and the national leaders recognised the equal social position of women with men. Several measures were taken by the successive governments to assign equal status to women in the economic, political and social fields. More avenues were opened to them to show their talents and have a sense of participation in national activities. The passage of several Acts by the Parliament and introduction of various schemes by the central as well as state governments during the last few decades have done much for women's emancipation legally, politically and socially. Education has also created awareness about opportunities outside of marriage, giving her financial independence and reducing her dependence on 'the man in her life' be it father or husband.

She now no longer needs to tolerate domestic violence or mental abuse at home. Health is also one of the area where woman suffers. Most women have neither the time nor the mind set or facilities to go in for healthcare. Rural women, specially, have no access to even such a basic healthcare facility as a toilet in their homes. Women's health is, therefore, a priority for government policies, with governments initiating programmes like 'Beti Bachao, Beti Padhao' and 'Janani Shushu Suraksha Karyakaram' etc. Social stigma related to single women whether widows, divorcees or unmarried women have also been one of factors for the poor status of women in India.

With women population being around 50 percent of the total population of the world, they have every right to be treated equally with men in every sphere of life. The inclusion of "Women Empowerment' as one of the prime goals in the eight Millennium Development Goals underscores the relevance of this fact. Swami Vivekananda's quote that, "There is no chance for the welfare of the world unless the condition of women is improved. It is not possible for a bird to fly on only one wing" beautifully sums up the essence of power of women in leading not just their families but also the nation and the world.

Feminist Theory-

Liberal feminist theory suggests that women are disadvantaged relative to men due to overt discrimination and/or to systemic factors that deprive them of vital resources like business education and experience. Previous studies that have investigated whether or not women are discriminated against by lenders and consultants, and whether or not women actually do have less relevant education and experience, are consistent with a liberal feminist perspective.

Social feminist theory suggests that, due to differences in early and ongoing socialisation, women and men do differ inherently. However, it also suggests that this does not mean women are inferior to men, as women and men may develop different but equally effective traits. Previous entrepreneurship studies that have compared men and women on socialised traits and values are consistent with a social feminist perspective. These studies have documented few consistent gender differences, and have suggested that those differences that do exist may have little impact on business performance. (Reference)

While this interpretation of past findings is relevant to the question of if and how female and male entrepreneurs differ, there are still large gaps in our knowledge.

1. Women and Social Enterprises

In the areas of equal representation of women in social enterprise leadership and equal pay for female social entrepreneurs, India ranked 27th and 36th, respectively. Women's participation in social enterprise in which India lags behind developed countries. The positive recognition for the work of individual entrepreneurs like Ajaita Shah, who distributes solar-powered lamps and stoves in rural Rajasthan through her company Frontier Markets, is remarkable in the sector.

Social enterprises perform significantly better on gender ratios than the average mainstream enterprise in India. According to the World Bank's Enterprise Survey data, 8.9% of mainstream enterprises in India have a woman top manager and 2.8% have majority female ownership. Entrepreneurial learning occurs because of certain personal, social and environmentally driven motivational factors. Entrepreneurial learning helps in the development of personal, social, managerial and entrepreneurial competencies. These competencies are essential for the performance of an enterprise.

Twenty-four percent of the social enterprises are led by women, higher than the 8.9% female-led firms in mainstream business/ private sector firms. The highest proportion of female-led social enterprises is highest in South India (35%), followed by North India (31%), and West India (23%), whereas it is much lower in East India (8%) and North-East India (3%). There were several non-responses to this question in the North. The fact that the region has the lowest number of social enterprises overall means women entrepreneurs are fewer too.

The highest proportion of social enterprises are found in Maharashtra, West India (16%) followed by Karnataka, South India (15%). Delhi and Telangana each accounted for 8% of the responses followed by Uttar Pradesh (7%), West Bengal (7%), Tamil Nadu (5%), Gujarat (5%), Bihar (4%), Odisha (4%), and Rajasthan (4%).

India could employ a number of ways to get more women into social entrepreneurship. One was to do it is to nudging them towards social entrepreneurship right from the time they are in college. India does not make good use of its women workforce, let alone promote women entrepreneurship.

2. Social Enterprise as a Tool for Women's Empowerment Organisations

There are many organisations around the world focused on empowering women and girls through practical action, campaigning and advocacy. The Association for Women's Rights in Development (AWID), is an umbrella body with over 5,000 members across 164 countries. Social enterprise, in its broadest sense, is not a new approach for women's empowerment organisations, but its use is increasing due to a combination of factors including a changing funding environment, a push from donors for financially sustainable models, and a growing awareness of the opportunities that social enterprise affords.

We found social enterprise being used by traditional women's empowerment organisations:

- As a source of funding for women's rights;
- As a means to deliver training or employment opportunities for women; and

- As a way to create economic empowerment through micro-entrepreneurship.
- The median income of women's rights organisations across the world is just $20,000. Forty eight percent of these organisations have never received core funding. Within this context, 29 percent of women's rights organisations have started to use income generating strategies and 17 percent have never received external funding. This is social enterprise as a survival strategy: social enterprise as a means to fund work on women's rights that no one else is willing to fund. Such social enterprise activity can help provide women's rights organisations by providing a basic level of financial security and autonomy over resources. However, it does not presently account for a very large amount of their overall income and over two-thirds of women's rights organisations globally have yet to adopt it as part of their strategy. It is an approach that is under-utilised and, where it is employed, could be more effective.

The use of a social enterprise approach to support women's economic empowerment has a relatively long history, particularly in India. Self-Employed Women's Associations bring together women working in the informal sector in the area of handicraft production. And self-help groups, often facilitated by NGOs, use microfinance and cooperative models to encourage micro-entrepreneurship among women.

Many NGOs working internationally have used this model under the banner of fair trade, providing a market for handmade products and providing a source of income for individual artisans, predominantly women.

Women's organisations are using social enterprise to raise funds and empower women directly through skill development, employment and the creation of economic opportunities. Although there are some limitations on the use of social enterprise for women's empowerment, many of these can be overcome through government legislation and public education. And despite these limitations, social enterprise is being used very effectively as a tool to empower women and girls.

3. Women as Social Entrepreneurs and Social Enterprise Leaders

There are differences in the impact on women of setting up a social enterprise from scratch and taking over the leadership of an established social enterprise, particularly in terms of the financial risk and compensation. Social enterprise is a young sector and most women leaders of social enterprises are also the founders, but that is not always the case, particularly for larger or more established social enterprises.

For- profit entrepreneurs and social entrepreneurs share some common characteristics but also exhibit important differences. Social enterprise was seen as a more flexible working option than any other sector by social entrepreneurs in every country. Women who need to provide an income for their families are not generally becoming social entrepreneurs themselves, but may benefit from employment opportunities created by social enterprises. In India, women can also struggle to secure support from their families, especially in the initial stages of becoming a social entrepreneur, and they face additional legal restrictions.

Unlike men, women are not usually expected to be the primary earner in the family. They may therefore have more freedom to take economic risks and accept lower pay or financial loss in their effort to start a social enterprise. And women can more easily engage with other women (especially in rural settings, where separation of the genders is more pronounced) for the purposes of bringing them into the social enterprise as beneficiaries, customers, employees, and/or affiliate microentrepreneurs.

4. Interviews with Entrepreneurs and Academicians

To understand the views of academicians and women entrepreneurs, we have interviewed some of the women entrepreneurs to get to know their perspectives field and the challenges regarding entrepreneurship.

(i) Prof Satish Agnihotri- Ex. IAS, Head CITRA and Centre for Policy Research, Indian Institute of Technology, Bombay, India: Prof. Agnihotri mainly discussed about Social Entrepreneurship and women empowerment. According to him, social enterprise-is one which does not shy away from profit making but keeps away from profit tearing. Social enterprises which would be developed in India will empower women that means involving more and more women in social enterprises but one thing which is important to make sure is that women should get access to revenue.

If women is involved in production making then they should be allowed for marketing too. There should be power symmetry between men and women. Kaplan Rai's article of Tamil Nadu on throws light how women who are employed in fish market their number decreases from retailers to sub- wholesaler to wholesalers hence this power asymmetry should be broken. If we look at the traditional basis then we get to see that subsidence work is done mainly by women and surplus production lies in the hand of men. Hence, if we are talking on women empowerment then we should engage women in surplus production not in subsidence labour.

Women should become social entreprenurs by choice but not by compulsion. According to him, there is a need in the society to make girls habituated in education and work sector.

(ii) Dr. Subhash Sharma- Director, Indus Business Academy, Bangalore: We interviewed Dr. Sharma during month of October 2018. Dr. Subhash Sharma is a leading Indian Management thinker and author of wellknown creative and thought provoking books like *"Creation from Shunya", "Management in New Age: Western Windows Eastern Door", "Quantum Rope: Science, Mysticism & Management", "New Mantras in Corporate Corridors", New Earth Sastra and Wisdom & Consciousness from the East: Life, Living & Leadership* (French translation, Leadership Par La Sagesse & La Conscience). His academic contributions have been acknowledged as 'creative and original' with 'quite a few exciting, nontraditional and revolutionary points of view' (Business Standard). As an Innovative Experimenter, Prof. Subhash Sharma has been experimenting with innovative approaches to teaching and learning such as the idea of Poetic methodology to teach management and leadership concepts through his well known 'Corporate Rhymes' and 3D (Discussion, Dialogue and Discourse) model of learning. His innovations have drawn print and Television media attention.

Dr. Sharma suggested the four models of women empowerment through social entrepreneurship:

- To include social entrepreneurship studies in universities.
- Creating social initiatives for example creation of self-help groups.
- Political model-laws and rules of the government and involvement and participation of women in panchayats and political arena.
- Spiritual presence of women for example right now it's just Brahma Kumari where women presence is there.

He gave a model known as swaswathika model of empowerment- which explains about restoring the balance men and women as men represents the violence side of nature and women represents the nonviolence side of the nature. Self empowerment is very important. With self-empowerment there are others also who need to be empowered. Other can be enemy, brother/sister, or reflection. For example, Mee Too Movement is an example of paradigm shift. Any situation in the society is influenced by following factors-

- Controllable-what is internal to one person
- Non-controllable-what is external to one.

Hence there are sides of decision-making which controllable and other one which is not controllable.

The question of empowerment which lies in non-controllable side of decision-making where women are dominated and they do not have their own decision-making power. In age of globalisation some other institution is also effecting in decision-making process, for example, autonomy. Therefore it's important to restore and give autonomy to women and hence it will lead to women empowerment. Some of the various models discussed with him which provide empowerment and how there is shift in the vision are as follows-

- Competitive model-in field of management
- Cooperation model-conferences which are organised
- Connectivity model that when one moves to brother or sister i.e. when one moves towards support.

According to him there is need to change from the system of super power to sadhvik system of the power where everyone has the power and autonomy to take decisions and hence there is a need to create harmonic society, secro-secular view of the world and Enlightened leadership apart from the only democratic model.

(iii) Prof Vibhuti Patel, Prof. at Tata Institute of Social Science, Mumbai in the Advanced Centre for Women's Studies: She promotes women entrepreneurship by teaching, training, writing, research and action. She agrees Feminist Theories of consciousness knowledge and collective wisdom, cocreation of knowledge are applicable to current situation. She spreads awareness about work by organising capacity building workshops, for example, e-pathashalas lectures, sharing her thoughts on social media. Government initiatives like gender responsive, participatory budgeting for women's education, employment, health and skill are promoting and playing crucial role in empowering women. Some of the suggestions made by her–

- Capacity building workshops in frontline areas in labour market are needed. Platform should be provided in all spheres of verticals be it economy, artificial intelligence, cloud computing, robotics etc.
- Move towards "women's haat" in the cities so that self-employed women get platform to improve their businesses.

(iv) Dr. Sangeeta Jhori, Prof at Rabindra Nath Tagore University at Bhopal, and she also works for rural women entrepreneur. In 2017, RNTU, Bhopal have started with Society for Unearthing Women Intellectual and Deep-rooted Holistic Aspiration (Swavidha) NGO which words according to the need analysis of the area nearby (Raisan, Bhopal). It is a NGO which was started by seven women which are working as faculties in the Rabindra Nath Tagore University. They have adopted five villages and working on those villages for women. They are associated with scheme–Unnat Bharat Abhiyan. The University provide customised training to the women entrepreneurs and so far the group of faculty members of RNTU, university, Bhopal they have empowered 1600 women.

(v) Dr. Sangeeta G. Naik, Principal, Achievers, Post Graduate College, Kalyan, India: Dr. Naik, has been influenced with the path of Gandhi ji. She proposed in institution to teach more about Gandhian Philosophy and his trustship Model. She advocate about the principals and methods of governance which can be applied in today's environment. She has also proposed that there is necessity to associate with women empowerment, self-reliance through Gandhian principle for holistic development of society.

(vi) Mrs. Vaishali Maple, Vice President, Prabha Engineering Pvt Limited- Mr. Vaishali shared that this startup started and promoted by her grandmother. She runs a startup which was started by her grandmother sixty years back. Her grandmother funded 8 thousand initially. She provided funding by cutting bitternuts after walking 2 to 3 kms. They are manufacturing organisation. They are breaking the taboo that women cannot work in manufacturing sector and shop floor.

Ms. Vaishali, feels that empowerment does not mean that taking or achieving something by force or by fear. She advocate dignity, love and shared values which make strong relations and support women in parts of life.

(vii) Mr. Amit Jain, Founder Mitti ke Rang, NGO in Pune: Mr. Amit Jain, Founder Mitti ke Rang, a NGO working for widow women. Mr. Jain started this NGO in 2014 and he is working for empowering widow women and single women. He explained that he is motivated by this idea as his own mother is a widow, and she has faced lots of criticism after death of her husband. Hence he wants to build a platform for ladies who can stand in her own strengths and become self-dependent.

Mitti Ke Rang means "color of soils", "because as a founder of this NGO, we consider that together we are stronger. MKR presents a platform of information and a network of partnerships between all the actors."

Mitti ke Rang provide project advocacy in 10 countries and also inculcate the entrepreneurship in widow women and teaching them embroidery and packaging (paper and bag making). **Mitti ke Rang** works with commonwealth. They do not take funding from government because of the ups and downs rather than they believe in crowd funding. Most of the women believe in doing the job rather than starting their own enterprises because of funding and money issues.

5. Case of National Bank for Agriculture and Rural Development (NABARD)

This case study seeks to analyse the role and contributions of an apex level bank specialising in agriculture and rural development programmes in India (NABARD) in creating a foundation and enabling environment for creating and sustaining social enterprises (SE). This institution has a diverse range of activities, from lending to sustainability. It is therefore, a unique institutional innovation in the agriculture and rural development sector on which nearly 70 percent Indian population depend for their livelihood. Also, both these segments of the Indian economy have been suffering from chronic poverty, unemployment, poor infrastructure and lack of modern irrigation facilities, inadequate credit and several other deficiencies (NABARD, 2016).

One of the objectives of this case study is to comprehend the role of institutional environments in creating and sustaining social enterprises in India; since not any and every institution in the financial sector can do it. In their publications, NABARD does not explicitly mention the types of social enterprises they have created, but the nature of organisations created and sustained either through alliance or direct funding or refinancing do indicate their direct and indirect contributions in these field. Further, NABARD, by way of encouraging innovations in agriculture and rural development fields has assumed a leadership role in the financial sector both in India and abroad. This case study identifies several types of institutional innovations which have resulted in the formation of social enterprises in dispersed locations in India. The case study also raises important questions on public policy and regulatory framework for financing social sector entrepreneurship in India. The case study offers inferences from the lessons of the various experiences of NABARD in promoting social enterprises.

(a) Sustainable development role of NABARD in terms of Economic, Social and Environmental goals.

Table 7.1: NABARD and Sustainable Development Goals

SDGs	*NABARD's Interventions*
No Poverty	SHG-Bank Linkage Programme, JLGs
	TDF, Wadi, Watershed
	UPNRM
	Farm Sector Promotion Fund, PODF, PRODUCE Fund, Farmers' Clubs
	RIDF projects – employment and income generation
	Financial Inclusion
Zero Hunger	SHG-Bank Linkage Programme, JLGs
	Credit facilities to federations for food security
Good Health and Wellbeing	SHG-BLP Livelihood interventions
	Tribal Development Programme
Quality Education	RIDF – social sector projects - schools
	Skill Development Programme, REDP, MEDP
Gender Equality	SHG-Bank Linkage Programme – WSHGs, Bank Sakhi Model, E-Shakti
	UPNRM
Clean Water and Sanitation	RIDF – social sector projects In-house energy, waste treatment and disposal
	RIDF – Social sector projects
Affordable and Clean Energy	NIDA – Clean and renewable energy projects
	SHG – BLP – Promotion of Green Energy
Decent Work and Economic Growth	SHG-BLP – Livelihoods
	Tribal Development Programme
Industry, Innovation and Infrastructure	RIDF, WIF, NIDA, FPF
	Rural Innovation Fund
	Off-Farm Sector Promotion Fund
Reduced Inequalities	SHG – BLP
	Financial Inclusion
	UPNRM, PODF, PRODUCE Fund
Sustainable Cities* and Communities ***NABARD's interventions cover only rural areas**	Climate Change Actions
	RIDF and NIDA – community engagements
Responsible Consumption and Production	In-house energy consumption
Climate Action	NIE for AF & GCF of UNFCCC & GoI's NAFCC
	Watershed Development, UPNRM
	Tribal Development
	RIDF & NIDA
	SHG-BLP – MEDP on renewable energy
Life Below Water	Refinance for Fisheries projects
Life on Land	SHG-BLP Livelihoods
	Refinance for dairy, poultry projects
	GoI's capital investment subsidy schemes for animal husbandry

(*Contd...*)

Peace, Justice and Strong Institutions	SHG-BLP
	Institutional Development of RRBs and cooperative credit institutions
Partnerships for the Goals	Stakeholder engagement – GoI, RBI, banks, MFIs, NGOs, SHGs, FPOs, International funding agencies – KfW, GIZ, etc., research institutions

Source: Authors compilation from NABARD Literature.

(b) NABARD E–Shakti: Pathway to Economic Empowerment of Women NABARD's Initiative

Self-Help Groups

In the year 1987, NABARD initially sanctioned ₹ 10 lakh to MYRADA [Mysore Resettlement and Development Agency] as financial assistance for experimenting on credit management crop. Along with this initiative, the Ministry of Rural Development started with the project of SHGs to provide finance by recognising the needs of the needy. (NABARD)

Thus, after the success of the Grameen microfinance model, the concept of Self Help Group (SHGs) gained momentum, which later was linked to banks through the SHG- Bank Linkage programme (BLP). (NABARD)

SHG was a pilot project of NABARD and was started in the year 1992 to curb the practices of approaching moneylenders for credit. It included a partnership of 3 agencies together namely: (1) SHGs (2) Banks and (3) NGOs.

After reviewing the working of the group in the year 1995, it allowed RBI to make a concrete decision of setting guidelines for

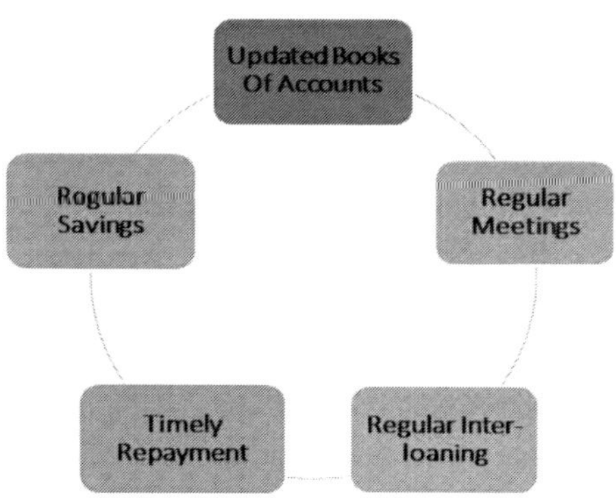

Figure 7.1

banks to enable SHGs to open a simple bank account on the agreement. NABARD created the linkage of the SHGs with the banks. Initially in the year 1992, it started with a slow growth rate, but later on, it increased gradually covering more than 39,995 members including both males and females.

(NABARD)

Till the 90s, a large group of underprivileged members of the village were dependent on money-lenders as the source of credit. Besides, one of the major issues was that they had poor maintenance of record and were left with a massive amount of debt and high-interest rate. The primary reason was the asymmetric information about the money being borrowed. Thus, to eliminate the monopoly of informal sources of finance, it was necessary to establish and expand self-help groups. This programme was designed to reach the masses, to bring maximum involvement of the people and make credit facilities available to them.

(c) National Rural Livelihood Mission

Under State Livelihood Mission of Deendayal Antyodya Yojana, also known as National Rural Livelihood Mission, the government aims to bring poor households into the banking system through mobilising bank credit. Under NRLM, it provides the Revolving Fund (RF) and the Community Investment Fund (CIF) for strengthening the financial aspect in the rural area.

(d) SHGs and BLP

SHGs and BLP have been successfully able to empower specifically the rural women. Taking the leap from 1992, SHGs have now become one of the largest microfinance community based on microfinance with 85.77 lakh SHGs in March 2017, covering the major portion of the SHGs. During the year 2016-2017, there was an increase of 6.73%. Yet, there was a need to connect 70.04 % poor houses in the less developed sector by connecting them through SHGs – BLP. (Ajeevika)

(e) SHGs in Digital World

Embracing the technology of smooth and efficient data flow and information, the SHGs were left out and failed to maintain a record of data. Soon there was an understanding that the SHGs should not be left out and there was a need to maintain the records and the data more systematically and the urge to convert SHG data into digital records.

Digitisation will be systematic and set faster-paced goals of the SHGs. Considering the problems, NABARD attempted digitisation under their project E-SHAKTI making most of the available information to maintain the records and improving the loopholes of the SHGs.

To overcome this problem and strengthen the SHG initiative, NABARD initiated a pilot project of E-SHAKTI in the year 2015, 15th March (where E- stands for electronic and SHAKTI means to empower), along with the Prime Minister's move with a digital India. It is a project where NGOs, organisations and banks come work together for achieving rural empowerment and prosperity of women. (NABARD)

The project E-SHAKTI helps in mapping down the existing SHGs in districts, by capturing all the data through its mobile app and tablet or to its dedicated website https://eshakti.nabard.org/ In case of failure, there is an alternate solution of uploading data that can be done offline. This data can be accessed by government agencies, NGOs and banks.

The government allocated ₹ 1.13 million for this programme by integrating the government department and the people for effective governance by transforming India into digital empowered society and knowledge economy. SHGs and bank linkage programme is a robust intervention in economic and financial inclusion from the bottom of the pyramid. Besides, it also helped in increasing the savings with the bank account and an increase in amount disbursement.

Table 7.2

Particulars	***Villages***
Villages Covered	19100
Groups Covered	1,30,000
Groups Credit Link	63,700
Members Covered	14,94,300
Women Covered	14,62,600
Members With Aadhar	12,07,700
Members Having Mobile Phones	51,15,800
Participating Banks	175
Participating Shpi	91

https://eshakti.nabard.org/

6. Akanksha Foundation, Chinchpokli, Mumbai

The Akanksha Foundation is a charitable organisation located at Chinchpokli in Mumbai. Ms Shaheen Mistry founded it in 1991. This foundation mainly works in the education sector by promoting education to children of low-level income families in the metro region of Mumbai and city like Pune. They work under a public-private partnership with 10 schools in Mumbai and 11 schools in Pune. They are self-funded private organisation working with government schools. They work to bring holistic transformation among children such as introducing dance, drawing and sports programme (also gender education) along with education.

This NGO was selected because it provides education and training programme to the women of the SHG group by linking various SHG together and improving the livelihood of the women by employing them. Thus, to understand their mechanism of empowering women, Mr. Rakesh Suresh Ghone was interviewed. Mr Rakesh is Senior Manager of Social Work at the NGO.

They have programme called SMC – School Management Committee program where they have a monthly discussion, between school teachers and the parents where they are enlightened about what decision is taken for the best interest of their children, academic plans etc. Besides they have a monthly parent-teachers meeting, counselling, empowering parents, upgrading their child nurturing skills, spreading the awareness about the education system.

Soon, they realised along with child education; there is a need for empowering women as 90% of women are involved and responsible in children's schooling. Most of them are illiterate (in the area where the foundation functions) and dependent on family for taking a decision and for empowering women it is essential to bring changes in prevailing male dominance in the society and to generate equality. The NGO is linked with various local NGO's. It has helped them to form a group of 50 parents in each area of Mumbai like Lower Parel and Worli slums.

To define the attitude of values and behaviour for empowerment, it is essential to bring changes through different training programmes. The organisation has developed a first training session for the new group of women where training is designed as per their need.

The organisation has made a structure with specific objectives to empower women who are:

- To develop linkages with NGO centres for delivering free training sessions on health, child adolescence and financial knowledge.

- To identify which programmes can be adopted for promoting for empowering women.
- To make efforts in organising the women for addressing their problems and difficulties.
- To help in managing their stress and pressure that they receive from family and society and help other women in problem.
- Having monthly inspection about the mid-day meals, uniforms.
- Involving women participation in schooling.
- Creating awareness about the education system among mothers.
- Empowering women as decision makers.
- Educating the illiterate women.
- Creating a job for the jobless women by providing them with skill training such as tailoring, beautician and basic computer skills.

(a) Initiatives

(1) They started with the programme called '**Muskan Har Ek Chehre Pe**' by providing them with capacity building training, health check-up, personality development, income generation tutorials, and mental health issues. The programme was divided into three years wherein the 1st year they focused on increasing the capacity building in women by providing them with information about the laws and legal rights of women, health and mental health. 2nd year was dedicated to providing them skill training such as computer training, tailoring and beautician not focusing on earning prospective but learning perspective. In the 3rd year, women were thought about cooking classes, seasonal cooking, putting up stalls celebrating the women sports day, these women had saving prospective so started with a women self-help group.

(2) SHG's programme was initiated with the wife of mill workers in Mumbai. They have tied up with many organisations such as Animet, Kamgar Mahila Sangh etc. where they provide need-based training to the women for generating income among them.

These several programmes have helped women to overcome the difficulties and started with the concept of women empowering through SHGs. The organisation further has tied up with 'Reliance Foundation'. They believe that women are more capable than men and are more dynamic when it comes to working. Given proper training or providing them with a primary support system the women shows uncountable results. Under this structure, the organisation has to provide training of more than 200 women within 1 year.

After the implementation of the programme, the foundation observed the following transition in the behaviour of women. The same was discussed during the interview.

Table 7.1 Transition after intervention of Akanksha Foundation

- Empowered women used their talent for improving their livelihood of self and society.
- Improved quality of education in government schools.

Table 7.3

	Before the training programme	*After the training programme*
1.	Trapped in the traditional customs and rituals	Ability to understand between good and evil and not following blindly under the name of tradition and customs
2.	Accepted that men run the society	Women are equal to men with common goals
3.	Pressurised to follow and implement what her family accepts	Learnt to place her own choice in front
4.	Unable to move outside their house without permission and restricted to work	Able to move out of their house without permission and work.

(b) Important points

(1) To merge with various NGO to cover a broad area

(2) Deliver training as per needs

(3) Financial independents

(4) Breaking stereotype of working women

7. Bharatiya Stree Shakti, Santacruz, Mumbai

Bharatiya Stree Shakti is at Vakola, Santacruz (BSS). It works for the holistic development of the society through empowering women to achieve dignity and self-respect for women by reducing gender inequality which they achieve by empowering women through skill training, financial and their health. The organisation has its founding members who belong to the different field so that they can acquire maximum knowledge from them to bring changes in the life of women. These consist of professors, social workers, lawyers, home-makers, bankers, doctors, engineers, mental health

भारतीय स्त्री शक्ति

Field visit at Bharatiya Stree Shakti, Mumbai

experts to provide maximum facilities and can solve problems at the earliest and give them a family environment; the organisation provides training based on their objectives.

The NGO was approached to understand how they provide solutions to women to come out to the problems by providing counselling session, empowerment training programme and market linkage programme. They engage maximum women in productive activity besides they have managed to create a market linkage programme and even manage to create a social norm creating unity among women themselves. The researcher interviewed Ms Urmila Apte, Co-founder of BSS and Nari Shakti Puraskar awardee.

(a) Mission

To transform women by improving health, education, economic independence, gender equality, self-esteem and decision-making participation.

(b) Objectives

(1) Job creation for women from all sections of the society.

(2) Promoting women and creating women-friendly at the workplace.
(3) Modern technology training for women.
(4) Setting up counselling centres like health, sanitation, water and childcare.

(c) **Insights from Ms Apte on Women Empowerment:** The first thing is to bring change in women to alter their cognitive pattern of considering herself equal to men by making them realise they are not a slave of their husbands firstly and secondly they are not bound with any believes and customs of the society. She adds that by their legal right women are equal to men and all living beings have equal position and dignity in the society.

She further added that over the years, BSS has been transforming the life of the women by making them aware of their constitutional rights and to understand themselves and rights.

(d) **Initiatives:** The researcher selected 20 representatives of 5 SHGs and based on focused group discussion; the results were that 25% of the women are engaged in food processing business as it is convenient for women to cook and have successfully started their own Tiffin service. They provide Tiffin services to the bank and other private organisations, and now they have ventured into the catering business.

Field visit at Bharatiya Stree Shakti, Mumbai

50% of the women are engaged in tailoring business because it requires lesser investment for the women. Through this women can work from home and manage their household work along with earning.

(e) **Self-Help Groups:** Women are first formed into SHG groups they are given capacity building training. These women belong to urban slum areas of central Mumbai. Most of the women who are part of the SHG of the group are illiterate or either attended only primary schools. The organisation provides them various type of training like financial education where women are given practical training and knowledge about the functioning of the bank and the process they need to know to open the account and to make them habituated. When asked about the loan procedure and repayment procedure, the beneficiaries reported the following:

15% of the women beneficiaries have a loan of ₹ 30,000 for 1 year from Vijaya Bank. The loan is taken to craft Diwali gifts. These women have manufactured more than 500 kgs of the handmade diyas and food for which they had tied up with different general stores of their locality.

5% of the women have taken a loan from SHG members as they wanted a loan for personal reasons like education and marriage with interest rate of 1% for 1 year or 2 years, the amount ranged between ₹ 50,000 to ₹ 80,000.

The SHG loan is to expand its existing business which contributes to financial autonomy. With this women are facilitating changes at the micro level which will lead to change in macro level by developing a feeling of unity and oneness. Besides this, they have control over economic aspects of controlling and producing goods and become a decision maker.

Cumulatively, the SHG's has distributed loans of ₹ 10,00,000 loans to women for various reasons out of which ₹ 8, 00,000 is already recovered.

One of the beneficiaries viewed that women do not prefer demanding loan from the bank as they have to follow the lengthy procedure.

Besides they also go through a mental pressure when they take the loan from the bank, that there is always a fear of "if they do not repay the loan then what circumstances they will have to undergo" this is the opposite scenario when the SHG grants loans to them.

She further added that their boundaries bind women; they create a wall which restraints themselves from doing anything. This will be broken only when they understand their inner power is much higher than the physical power.

(f) **Capacity Building Training:** To break this stereotype, BSS conducts capacity building programme for women, even if they are not part of the SHG group. The training that they provide aims in building self-awareness and self-confidence; to make them believe in themselves by giving them proper guidance and regular practice.

The outcome of this training is that it has helped 12% of the women to start their own business and 5% of the women have started taking classes or home tuitions for primary standards, and 2% have started taking lectures in classes on regular bases. These women dream of starting their classes or education centres for women and children.

The organisation provides raw material to the SHG women as these women do not have to store or invest money in purchasing raw material. The material is provided to them in bulk so that they can earn extra profit margin.

(g) **Outcomes:** The organisation has achieved specific parameters of women empowerment after forming SHGs and training they received:

(1) Raising self-confidence and self-esteem

(2) Elimination of discrimination

(3) Building independent women organisation

(4) Promoting unity along with creating positive imagine of the women in the society and among their group

(5) Collective action

(6) Collective working and analytical thinking.

Key Learnings: While much has been done to integrate women's experiences into development discourse and human rights, the condition and situation of the women in the world today seem indicates that the knowledge we have gained has not led to any improvement in their lives. In the organised manufacturing sector, though the number of jobs has grown, there has also been an increase in the share of contract work, which offers lower wages and less job security, according to the study.

Women social entrepreneurs share many characteristics with for-profit entrepreneurs. They the same barriers and enablers. Their motivations however are quite different, as social entrepreneurs are driven almost entirely by a desire to create social impact. Women social entrepreneurs face the same barriers as their male counterparts, and also additional barriers as a result of their gender. Becoming a social entrepreneur has a positive impact on women's self-confidence, sense of self-worth and power over her own decisions.

Chapter - 8

Recommendations and Policy Implications for Empowering Women through Entrepreneurship

A significant influence on women's ability to participate in the economy comes from social and political factors which includes access to family planning and other healthcare services; including social protection. This covers improving literacy rates of adult women; and, increasing women's influence in governance structures and political decision-making. The success of a country in empowering the women is highly dependent on the responsive and multifaceted approach of public policy management and implementation, including its macro-economic, financial and trade policies.

In this regards, Government of India has taken various initiatives and incorporates a perspective of gender equality into gender budgeting, which covers entire budget cycle from strategic planning to audit oversight. Social protection enriches the capability of deprived and vulnerable women to escape from poverty and to better cope up with risks and shocks. Social protection measures include social insurance, cash transfers and minimum labour standards.

Although the government has done a lot to increase the female participation in the labour force but government should also design policies to remove obstacles that make it difficult for women with children to work and provide other incentives. For reaping the economic benefits of more working women, countries should have mandated and funded family friendly policies to address the abnormalities. Well-designed vocational training leads to better paid work, and does not concentrate women only in low-wage and low-skill work or reinforce occupational segregation between women and men. For more effective poverty reduction, differential gender impacts programmes should be considered in the entire package of development activities to enhance women's opportunities through investments in livelihoods, infrastructure and legal rights as well as education and health.

Further policy-making is possible when data is made available which highlights the reasons of why women lack in accessing formal financial services. Advanced models which include qualitative variables like genders, behavioural aspects and cognitive models need to fully understand the reasons behind low financial inclusion. This would prompt the policy-makers to tackle it in the most effective manner and roll out plans targeting specific variables rather than a unified macro policy.

Creating conditions for gender empowerment demands that empowerment policies and programmes incorporate women's voice and agency as fundamental conditions. To ensure that women are heard at all levels — as individuals, in communities and nationally, empowerment must be defined in a manner appropriate for the task. If the goal is to understand the process that leads to empowerment, then we need definitions that can be theorised and empirically analyzed. These commitments must also recognize women as belonging to heterogeneous groups that suffer from discrimination and patriarchy and in a multiplicity of ways, in various localities, and times. When viewed in the broader context, gender empowerment will not be attained simply by listening to the voice of women and creating space for agency as this is not enough to end the marginalisation and entrenched patterns of discrimination against women. However, it is a step towards creating a vision that goes beyond merely paying lip service to women's needs. The challenge is to empower women in the construction of a new India, but this will not be achieved until the innate strength, knowledge and experience of 48 percent of the Indian population is fully engaged in gender empowerment goals.

The gender-sensitive approach in public policies – gender mainstreaming–creates the sincere opportunity to improve the role of women enterprises, to understand their disadvantages and to eliminate the barriers in front of them. This requires simultaneous interventions. Government should declare manifestations in order to proclaim the values, to eliminate the prejudices, shaping the approach positively by means of deeds, actions like prizes, competitions, sponsorship programmes - with systematic initiatives aimed at women. Genuine changes are achievable in the field of eliminating the social and economic inequalities between the genders if every concerned participant simultaneously appears at all three levels.

Procedures and formalities should be simplified for registration of business, legal and financial assistance, concessions, subsidies, relief from government and non-governmental organisations. Women entrepreneurs should be encouraged to participate in trade fairs, conferences and exhibitions. Efforts should be made through governmental and nongovernmental organisations to create awareness about policies, strategies and schemes.

National level forums should be established to promote discussions on issues and grievances faced by women entrepreneurs and suggest probable policy framework to resolve the same.

1. Women Empowerment

1.1 Enhancing Opportunities for Women

Creating opportunities for women requires ensuring women's empowerment in the economic, political and cultural spheres. Investing in girls and women has multidimensional benefits— for example, if all girls in developing countries completed secondary education, the underfive mortality rate would

Factors that enable or constrain women's empowerment—six direct and four underlying factors

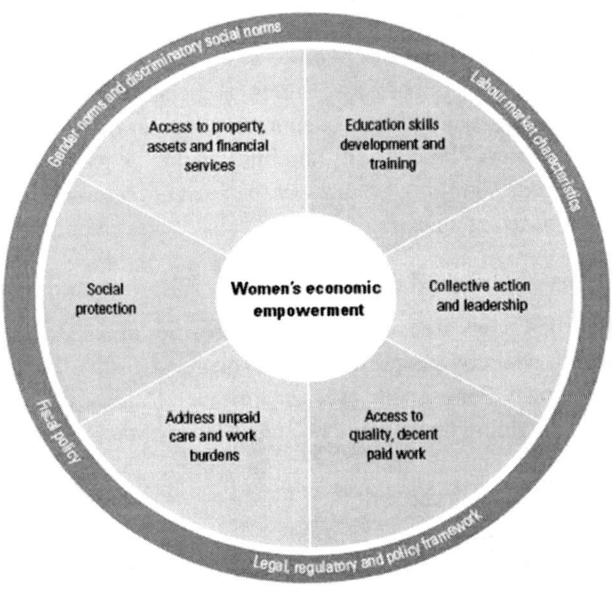

Source: Hunt and Samman 2016.

Diagram 8.1

be halved. More women should be in science, technology, engineering and mathematics, where much future demand for high-level work will be supported by women. Only one-fifth of countries had achieved gender parity in research by 2015, meaning that 45–55 percent of researchers were women. Increasing women's enrolment in tertiary education and science, technology, engineering and mathematics requires such incentives as scholarships, admission quotas and internships with research institutions.

1.2 Assessing Women Empowerment Framework

(a) **Identifying Constraints to Action:** Identifying constraints is a participative process. It contributes towards building an understanding among the women involved in how they are discriminated against on the basis of their gender.

(b) **Identifying how Women's Agency has Developed:** This is a mirror image to identifying constraints. If constraints to action are loosened then, by definition, possibilities for action (agency) are increased. Also, vice versa, if possibilities for action are increased then constraints have loosened.

However, the interest lies not only in possibilities for action but in actual action taken. Analysing changes in women's agency will involve considering both the individual and collective level.

(c) **Identifying How Women's Agency Changed Constraints to Action:** Impact assessment is determining whether observed changes are a result of an intervention or caused by some external factor. The necessity to consider this as part of the assessment exists in this case too, but the attribution question also has to be faced at an extra level when considering empowerment.

The Dis-aggregated Perspective

Disparities in one area may reinforce disparities in other areas and create a dynamic whereby people are left further and further behind in human development. For example, women are generally disadvantaged relative to men in obtaining the benefits of human development. If such women are living in ecologically fragile areas, they are doubly deprived: because of their gender and because of their location.

2. Gender and Sustainable Development: Broad Context

2.1 Economics and Gender

(i) **Women Labour Force Participation:** The discrimination towards women can be addressed through proposing changes in the legal structure, family codes and laws, increasing communication towards gender equity.

For more effective poverty reduction, differential gender impacts should be considered in the entire package of development activities to enhance women's opportunities through investments in livelihoods, infrastructure and legal rights as well as education and health (OECD, 2007).

(ii) **Women and Technology:** A government can make provision of monetary and non-monetary incentives to encourage women to participate in science and technology careers.

To attract women candidates to pursue technical education, grants, awards, scholarship can be given at university level as they are reluctant to engage in the technical jobs due to reconciling work and family responsibilities. In every career field, women should be allowed to enter professional careers at a later stage and work on flexible and temporary work contracts with family-friendly work practices, childcare and parental leave.

(iii) **Women and Management:** Stereotype towards women exists that they are not leadership material which has led to the decline in the proportion of women in senior roles.

Three types of interventions can help counteract these trends: (1) establishing and monitoring targets for women managers, (2) setting up networking and development programmes, and (3) ensuring family-friendly work practices.

Women are often excluded from informal networks and lack mentors and development experiences which limits their advancement. Policies should not be aimed towards helping women adapt to a male-centered work environment, but rather to promoting changes in organisations to discourage gender stereotyping (Wittenberg-Cox, 2008).

(iv) **Women Entrepreneurs:** Steps should be taken to simplify the path of women entrepreneurs; the government should increase targeted financing and training. Some of the governments are undertaking programmes to accelerate learning in assessing entrepreneurial risk as well as promoting special lending programmes for women which includes increasing credit lines to women entrepreneurs through the medium of commercial banks. Micro-finance is one of the most effective ways to empower women and increase their access to sustainable livelihoods and economic assets.

Networking programmes and programmes where training is given through experienced women professional help the potential entrepreneur. Initiatives to foster women entrepreneurs should also be part of local development strategies and enterprise creation policies.

2.2 Society and Gender

(i) **Women and Education:** Educating females is essential to increasing productivity in all economies, particularly in the developing world where it depends in large part on engendered development assistance policies.

Guidance and counselling should be given to women so that they get information on the range of jobs to which they can apply based on the skills.

Traditional areas of female work including teaching, nursing and social services should be upgraded to reflect their real contributions to the economy and society.

Governments need to reassess the qualifications and skills needed for different types of jobs on a gender-neutral scale. Equal pay legislation does not solve the gender wage gap since it addresses only discrimination in similar jobs with the same employer.

(ii) **Women and Health:** Occupational health and safety practices should take into account gender-specific factors such as non-standard employment, home-based work, and contingent work performed by women.

The government should consider access to women in terms of education and improvements in primary healthcare including reproductive health. The aim should be at building government capacity to inculcate gender perspectives in development planning.

(iii) **Women and Governance:** Facilitating female participation in governance may depend on specialised training and information programmes to explain complex legal processes. Schemes to assist working parents with time constraints, as well as mentoring and networks, also help to give women new roles in political life.

Some countries have adopted quotas and targets for increasing women's representation in government and parliaments.

2.3 Women and Sustainability

(i) **Women and Sustainable Consumption:** Governments can build on female consumer preferences to promote more sustainable consumption patterns to benefit the economy and society. Initiatives for promoting sustainable consumption in certain product groups (energy, transport) could be directed to the lifestyles, attitudes and proclivities of the most likely group of consumers for which consumption behaviour of men and women is needed.

In surveys, women support more government intervention in the marketplace to promote sustainable consumption behaviour. They advocate bans on unsustainable products, lower prices for environmentally-friendly goods, and better labelling of the environmental and social impacts of products and their production. In the home, women support government grants to make green energy choices cheaper and more readily available, comprehensive recycling programmes and facilities, and more stringent standards for housing stocks and energy conservation.

(ii) **Women and Sustainable Production:** Governments can promote sustainable corporate production through the support of reporting systems and international instruments. More international codes of conduct should include reporting and monitoring on how a company's product range supports sustainable production all along the global supply chain.

More large companies are providing information in connection with global sustainability instruments and codes of conduct, including the OECD Guidelines for Multinational Enterprises, the UN Global Compact, and the Global Reporting Initiative (GRI). These are comprehensive frameworks which cover environment, social and corporate governance issues. Governments prescribe adherence to the OECD guidelines for their firms, including both environmental tenets ("enterprises should take due account of the need to protect the environment") and social tenets including gender (enterprises are expected to promote equal opportunities for women and men). Disputes may arise regarding nonadherence to the OECD Guidelines and, in this context, the status of women has been raised in relation to projects in the mining, oil and gas, and hydroelectric sectors as well as export processing zones (OECD, 2007).

(iii) **Women and Climate Change:** Technology transfer and Clean Development Mechanism (CDM) projects could be designed in a gender-sensitive way to promote the dual purpose of climate protection and enhancing the role of women.

3. Building Effective Women's Economic Empowerment Strategies by Various Organisations

While many agencies actively promote women's economic empowerment, most agencies have been approaching women's economic empowerment through isolated programmes and investments. These have led to some incremental improvements for women—as well as benefits to business—but the private sector has much more to offer and to gain for advancing opportunities for women.

Real transformation for women will happen when companies tackle the structural and systemic barriers standing in the way of women's economic advancement. Companies can achieve more significant impact and create more business value by employing a holistic and integrated approach, one that addresses underlying systemic barriers to women's economic empowerment and includes gender considerations across the entire company.

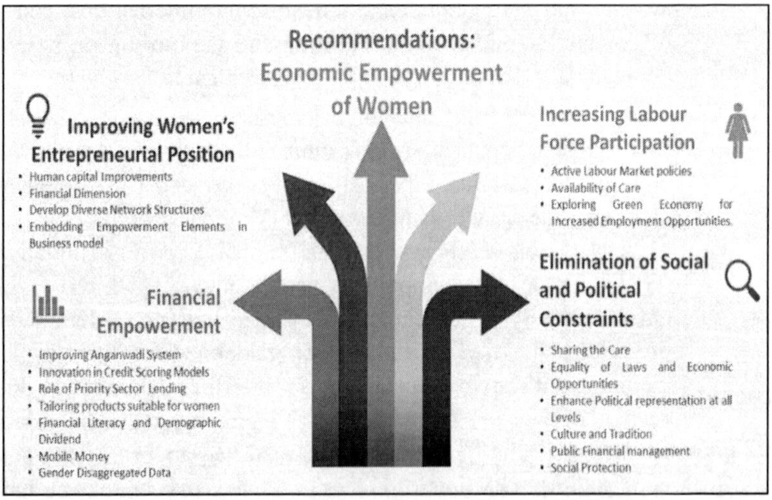

Diagram 8.2: Recommendations for Economic Empowerment of Women.

3.1. Policy Implications for Improving Women's Entrepreneurial Position

One key question that resonates throughout this study is what, if anything, can be done to influence the circumstances under which women entrepreneurs operate on a local, national and international level.

(i) **Human Capital Improvements:** In terms of human capital issues, women entrepreneurs need to have access to outlets that improve this resource for their entrepreneurial development. Such outlets could include more extensive training in development in areas related to owning one's own business.

(ii) **Financial Dimension:** Women with access to pension and savings in bank accounts are more capable of making independent decisions on resource use. Enhancing women's control over the resources increases their bargaining power in households (Duflo, 2012). There is also a strong relationship between women's financial inclusion and their performance as entrepreneurs in developing countries (OECD, 2012). Financial inclusion is considered as an essential tool to lessen poverty by promoting entrepreneurship and creation of jobs.

(iii) **Develop Diverse Network Structures:** In terms of network structures and their development for women entrepreneurs, there is a need to systematically address different aspects of this dimension, in order to adequately aid women entrepreneurs. First, women entrepreneurs need to pursue the development of smaller and more manageable network structures, so the qualities of their network structures are strengthened with very useful links.

(iv) **Training and Education:** Education is also one of the strongest determinants of real female entrepreneurship in India (Daymard and Sorsa, 2015). The focus of the Central and the State Government has been increasingly on skill-based training to create self-employment and a new army of female entrepreneurs. The rate of female entrepreneurship is lower in India concerning economic development; the low rate may be due to issues with the overall business environment.

3.2 Policy Implications for Increasing Participation in the Labour force

(i) **Active Labour Market Policies:** Skill development programmes have also been proven effective to make a difference. In India, one such programme is STEP which is initiated by the Ministry of Women and Child Development for assetless rural and urban women. Also, the private sector should also be encouraged to hire women at all levels.

(ii) **Availability of Care:** Prevalence of unpaid work is primarily attributed to a lack of affordable care facilities. Lack of care facilities for children and elderly persons from the family often results in lower participation in the labour force. However, having more females in the household may raise participation because other female relatives may take of the children and the elderly.

(iii) **Exploring Green Economy for Increased Employment:** India can adopt a model of European countries with respect to the green economy. Renewable energy, transport infrastructure, auto companies, and green buildings and factories are receiving an infusion of public money. However, this green growth may exacerbate social sustainability in ignoring widening income and gender gaps.

(iv) **Changing Paradigms:** In India, business leadership positions that are open to women are often limited to micro or small enterprises. In such contexts, policies promoting women's entrepreneurship and supporting the participation of women-led small and medium-sized enterprises in public sector procurement can be particularly relevant. Women's representation can be increased through affirmative action, such as quotas for women on corporate boards, as in the European Union. Such efforts are even more effective when accompanied by policies that raise retention rates. Mentoring, coaching and sponsoring can empower women in the workplace by using successful senior female entrepreneurs as role models and as sponsors. All these approaches can change norms and promote women to become more responsible.

(iv) **Recommendations in Non-Governmental Organisations Context**

- There is a need for greater collaboration, (Law enforcement media, individual level activists) the sharing of best practice and the replication of successful models. NGOs need to collaborate with business, bringing new expertise and deep relationships with stakeholders.
- Appropriate business support and funding for women could enable some of them to develop formal social enterprises and potentially earn an. income from their work. We can follow some of the best NGOs practices.

- More transparency, openness and accountability required by representing the exact figures and statics on the respective website of the NGOs on a quarterly basis. Developing strategies include the mechanism of consistent monitoring of whether they are implemented and linking it to the organisation's goal. There is a need to bolster public confidence in the voluntary sector by opening it to public scrutiny.
- Training materials and timely allocation of funds to the NGOs.
- The government could simplify and streamline the system for granting income tax exemptions status to charitable projects under the Income-tax Act as public donations play a crucial role in funding NGOs. At the sametime, tightening of administrative and penal procedures to ensure that paper charities do not misuse these incentives for their private financial gains.

Conclusion

The concept of women's empowerment is diverse, but the core ideas of all the concepts in the literature are concentrated around women's options, choices, control and power. The process of conceptualising and measuring women empowerment is challenging. Studies on women empowerment provides a foundation for measuring the progress of empowerment, which is beneficial in developing an operational roadmap for measuring women's empowerment. Thus, to simplify the process additional iterations need to take place to develop an approach viable for international development agencies.

Creating conditions for gender empowerment demands that empowerment policies and programmes incorporate women's voice and agency as fundamental conditions. Recognition must be given to the fact that women suffer from discrimination and patriarchy and in a multiplicity of ways, in various localities, and times. To ensure that women are heard at all levels — as individuals, in communities, and nationally, empowerment must be defined in a manner appropriate for creating the desired conditions.

It is inferred from the authors' review that many studies do not measure the process of empowerment effectively. Government, development agencies and researchers conclude that enabling factors such as education, employment, positive marriage or kinship conditions, or programmatic interventions such as microcredit lead to women having more choice, options, control, or power over their living conditions. In these studies, it is important to consider that factors that require subjective judgement.

Our study shows that Empowerment of Women can be assumed as 'Agents of Social Change and Development' if all the stakeholders of society can give equal importance to women as they give to men. There is a lack of confidence among women, which can be built if society shows faith on her.

Merely giving token participation in schemes or involving women in several government initiatives would only increase the statistics of women participation in the labour force. If the governments seek to empower in the truest sense, they must look at each of their schemes through the feminist lens. They must analyze how they can bring into the picture the confidence of the women. For instance, even though SHGs are helpful to self-employed women, some of the women are still having to fight battles from home before they come to work. The question then arises- what is economic empowerment without social empowerment? What does the State seek to achieve?

This study is an attempt at answering these questions. And a step in showing that when given the opportunity, women do utilise it to their maximum. This study was conducted from February 2018 to December 2018. During the entire discussion, field study and observation, it was observed that for supporting women to come forward and utilise all the opportunities created by government. Both government and society have to work together. The action is needed in various areas including institutional and non-institutional support.

Still in some sections, social discrimination is there, women continue to be excluded from participating in both public decision-making processes and also in decisions making about resource distribution, family size and income usage at the family level. This illustrates the lack of State accountability vis-à-vis the delivery of women's human rights, including development-related ones. This suggests that women are still undervalued. Might it not be time to move beyond rhetoric and yet more elaborate analyses of human rights to actually delivering them, and thereby honouring our collective humanity.

To bring women in the mainstream of the developmental activities of the country, it is vital to empower women economically and socially. The governments and development agencies consider increasing economic

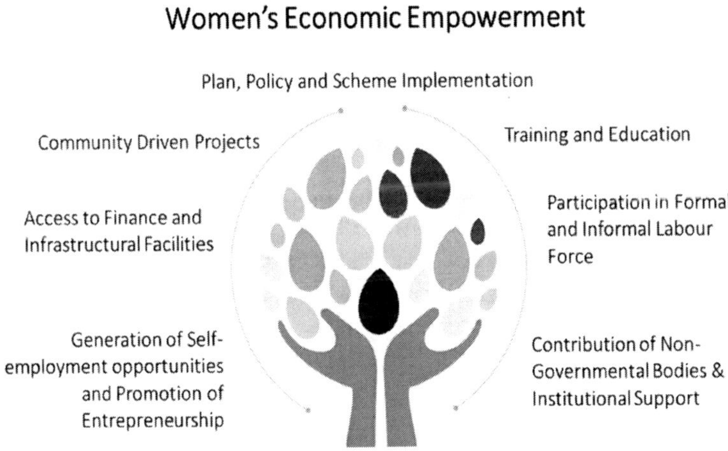

Diagram 8.3: Holistic Approach of Empowerment.

participation by participating in the labour force and promoting women entrepreneurship.

To ensure the provision of training, employment and income generation activities with both 'forward' and 'backward' linkages with the ultimate objective of making all potential women economically independent and self-reliant. In our case studies of MAVIM, NABARD, Udyogini, Bharatiya Stree Shakti, Care Foundation and a various similar organisations, it is observed and recorded that these organisations are supporting women by providing them financial and non-financial support.

Women's entrepreneurship can make a strong contribution to the economic wellbeing of the family and communities, poverty reduction and women's empowerment, thus contributing to the Sustainable Development Goals (SDGs). Thus, governments across the world, as well as various developmental organisations, are actively undertaking the promotion of women entrepreneurs through various schemes, incentives and promotional measures.

Despite consistent efforts to boost women's economic participation, the participation of women in the labour force is on the decline.

Women entrepreneurship has been recognised as an essential source of economic growth. Women entrepreneurs create new jobs themselves and others and also provide society with different solutions to management, organisation and business problems. Therefore, it is a sign that women contribute to society by engaging in social entrepreneurship. However, women social entrepreneurs still represent a minority of all entrepreneurs.

Therefore, what we really need, other than empowerment and collective action is a sense of confidence in the minds of the very oppressed population. A sense of being aware of the deprivations and yet a motivation to go beyond. Through this study we witnessed the potential of the women in these SHGs. It shows how women can successfully engage in collective entrepreneurship to achieve economic and social change.

References

Chapter 1

- Çagatay, N., Keklik, M., Lal, R., & Lang, J. (2000). Budgets as if people mattered: Democratizing macroeconomic policies. *Social Development and Poverty Elimination Division, Bureau of Development Policy.* New York: UNDP.
- Kanji, N., & Menon, K. (2001). *What does the Feminisation of Labour Mean for Sustainable Livelihoods? International Institute for Environment and Development.*
- Malhotra, A., Schuler, S. R., & Boender, C. (2002). Measuring Women's Empowerment as a Variable in International Development. In *background paper prepared for the World Bank Workshop on Poverty and Gender: New Perspectives* (Vol. 28).
- Rathgeber, E. M. (1990). WID, WAD, GAD: Trends in research and practice, *The Journal of Developing Areas,* 489–502S.
- Rosenfeld, R. A. (1996). Women's Work Histories. Population and Development Review, 22, 199-222.
- Sharma, A. (2008). Logics of Empowerment: Development, Gender, and Governance in Neoliberal India. U of Minnesota Press.
- Standing, G. (1999). *Global Labour Flexibility: Seeking Distributive Justice.* Palgrave Macmillan.
- Waterson, A. (1966). Development Planning. Lessons of Experience. *Development planning. Lessons of experience.*
- http://www.un.org/sustainabledevelopment/sustainable-development-goals/
- https://www.unfpa.org/
- http://yojana.gov.in/Yojana%20October%20(3).pdf%20-%20final.pdf
- https://www.oecd.org/dac/gender-development/47561694.pdf
- https://www.unwomen.org/en/csw
- https://www.unwomen.org/en/digital-library/publications/2018/2/gender-equality-in-the-2030-agenda-for-sustainable-development-2018
- http://www.unrisd.org/unrisd/website/projects.nsf/(httpProjects)/5F7EC3623063C8D180 256B5D00440321?OpenDocument
- https://www.unfpa.org/gender-equality
- Turning promises into action: Gender equality in the 2030 Agenda for Sustainable Development, https://www.unwomen.org/en/digital-library/publications/2018/2/genderequality- in-the-2030-agenda-for-sustainable-development-2018

Chapter 2

- Acharya, M., & Bennett, L. (1981). Rural Women of Nepal: An Aggregate Analysis and Summary of 8 Village Studies. Centre for Economic Development and Administration, Tribhuvan University.
- Allen, K. R. (2016). Feminist Theory in Family Studies: History, Biography, and Critique. *Journal of Family Theory & Review*, 8, 207– 224.
- Baden, S. and Oxaal, Z. (1997). Gender and Development Definitions, Approaches and Implications for Policy. *BRIDGE (Development-Gender) Brigton,* Institute of Development Studies, Report No. 40, 1-32.
- Bardhan, K., & Klasen, S. (1999). UNDP's Gender-related Indices: A Critical Review. *World Development*, *27*(6), 985-1010.
- Batliwala, S. (1993). Empowerment of Women in South Asia. Asian, South Pacific Bureau of Adult Education and FAO's Freedom from Hunger campaign/ Action for Development.
- Birkenmaier, J., & Berg-Weger, M. (2014). *The Practice of Generalist Social Work.* Routledge.
- Bisnath, Savitri and Diane Elson (2000). Women's Empowerment Revisited, a Background Paper for the United Nations Progress Report of the World's Women, A New Biennial Report. Electric document: http://www.undp.org/unifem/progressww/empower.html
- Chambers, R. (1997). Whose Reality Counts? Putting the First Last. *Rugby: Intermediate,* Technology Publications.
- Charmes, J., & Wieringa, S. (2003). Measuring Women's Empowerment: An Assessment of the Gender-related Development Index and the Gender Empowerment Measure, *Journal of Human Development*, *4*(3), 419-435.
- CIDA (Canadian International Development Agency) (1997). Guide to Gender-Sensitive Indicators. Quebec, Canada: CIDA. http://www.acdicida. gc.ca/INET/IMAGES.NSF/vLUImages/Policy/$file/WID-GUID-E.pdf.
- Dahl, R. A. (1957). The Concept of Power. *Behavioral Science,* 2(3), 201-215.
- Das, M. and S. Desai (2003). Why are Educated Women Less Likely to be Employed in India?, Social Protection Unit Discussion Paper No. 313. The World Bank, Washington DC. http://www.sonaldedesai.org/das_and_desai_2003_on_women.pdf
- Elias, M. J., Ferrito, J. J., & Moceri, D. C. (2016). The Other Side of the Report Card: Assessing Students' Social, Emotional, & Character Development. Thousand Oaks, CA: Corwin.
- Gage, A.J. (1995). Women's Socioeconomic Position and Contraceptive Behavior in Togo. *Studies in Family Planning* 26(5): 264-277.
- Graham, C., and S. Pettinato. (2005). "Subjective Well-Being and Objective Measures: Insecurity and Inequality in Emerging Markets." In Measuring Empowerment: Cross-Disciplinary Perspectives, ed. D. Narayan. Washington, DC: World Bank.
- Gupta, K., & Yesudian, P. P. (2006). Evidence of Women's Empowerment in India: A Study of Socio-spatial disparities. *Geo Journal*, *65*(4), 365-380.

- Jagannathan, S. (1999). The Role of Nongovernmental Organisations in Primary Education: A Study of Six *NGOs in India*. The World Bank.
- Jejeebhoy S., (2000). Women's Autonomy in Rural India: Its Dimensions, Determinants, and the Influence of Context. In Harriet B. Presser and Gita Ser (eds.), Women's Empowerment and Demographic Processes: Moving Beyond Cairo, New York, Oxford University Press.
- Jejeebhoy, S. J., & Sathar, Z. A. (2001). Women's Autonomy in India and Pakistan: The Influence of Religion and Region. *Population and Development Review*, *27*(4), 687-712.
- Kabeer, N. (1999). Resources, Agency, Achievements: Reflections on the Measurement of Women's Empowerment, Development and Change, Vol. 30, pp. 435-464.
- Kabeer, N. (2001). Conflicts Over Credit: Re-evaluating the Empowerment Potential of Loans to Women in Rural Bangladesh. *World development*, *29*(1), 63-84.
- Keller, B. and B. Mbwewe (1991). Policy and Planning for Empowerment of Zambian Women Farmers, *Canadian Journal of Development Studies,* 12 (1), pp. 75-88.
- Kishor, S. (2000). Empowerment of Women in Egypt and Links to the Survival and Health of their Infants. In H. Presser & G. sen (Eds.), Empowerment and Demographic Processes: Moving Beyond Cairo (pp. 20-24). New York: Oxford University Press.
- Kritz, M. M., P. Makinwa-Adebusoye, and D.T. Gurak (2000). The Role of Gender Context in Shaping Reproductive Behaviour in Nigeria, in Women's Empowerment & Demographic Processes, Harriet B. and Gita Sen Presser. New York: Oxford University Press.
- Kumar and Paul (2017). Women Empowerment: Challenges and Strategies, Om Publications.
- Liranso G Selamu and Mohan S Singhe (2017). The Psycho-social Empowerment of Women: A Critical Review, *EC Psychology and Psychiatry* 5.1 08-15.
- Luttrell, C. and S. Quiroz (2007). 'Understanding and Operationalising Empowerment'. *ODI paper for the SDC Poverty- Wellbeing Platform.*
- Luttrell, C., Quiroz, S., Scrutton, C., & Bird, K. (2009). Understanding and Operationalizing Empowerment (pp. 1-16). London: Overseas Development Institute.
- Malhotra, A., Vanneman, R., & Kishor, S. (1995). Fertility, dimensions of Patriarchy, and Development in India. *Population and Development Review*, 281-305.
- Malhotra, A., Schuler, S. R., & Boender, C. (2002). Measuring Women's Empowerment as a Variable in International Development. In B*ackground Paper Prepared for the World Bank Workshop on Poverty and Gender: New Perspectives* (Vol. 28).
- Markham, S. (2013). Women as agents of Change: having Voice in Society and Influencing Policy.
- Mason, Karen (1986). The Status of Women: Conceptual and Methodological Issues in Demographic Studies, *Sociological Forum 1*(2): 284-300.

- Mayoux, L. (2000). *Micro-finance and the Empowerment of Women: A Review of the Key Issues* (No. 993441343402676). International Labour Organisation.
- Mosedale, S. (2003). Towards a Framework for Assessing Empowerment (No. 1652-2016-136010).
- Mosedale, S. (2005). Assessing Women's Empowerment: Towards a Conceptual framework. *Journal of international development*, *17*(2), 243-257.
- Narayan, Deepa, and Talat Shah. 2000. Gender Inequity, Poverty, and Social Capital. Policy Research Report on Gender Development, Working Paper Series. Washington, D.C.: World Bank.
- Pitt, M. M., & Khandker, S. R. (1998). The Impact of Group-Based Credit Programs on Poor Households in Bangladesh: Does the Gender of Participants Matter? *Journal of Political Economy*, *106*(5), 958-996.
- Rao, Viajyendra (1998). Wife-abuse, its Causes and its Impact on Intra-household Resource Allocation in Rural Karnataka: A 'Participatory' Econometric Analysis, in Gender, Population and Development, Maithreyi Krishnaraj, Ratna M. Sudarshan, and Ausaleh Shariff, eds. Delhi, Oxford, and New York: Oxford University Press.
- Rowlands, J. (1998). A Word of The Times, But What Does It Mean? Empowerment in The Discourse & Practice of Development. In *Women and Empowerment* (pp. 11-34). Palgrave Macmillan, London.
- Sell, M. and Minot, N. (2018). What Factors Explain Women's Empowerment? Decision-Making Among Small-Scale Farmers in Uganda, *Women's Studies International Forum*, Vol. 71, pp. 46-55.
- Sen, A. (1990). Gender and Cooperative Conflicts. In: Tinker I. (eds). Persistent Inequalities: *Women and World Development.* Oxford University Press, New York.
- Scott, J. W. (1986). Gender: A Useful Category of Historical Analysis. *The American Historical Review,* 91(5), 1053-1075.
- Sen, A. (1999). Development as Freedom. Oxford: Oxford University Press.
- Stromquist, N. (1993). The Practical and Theoretical Bases for Empowerment. In I*nternational Seminar on Women's Education and Empowerment, UNESCO Institute for Education, Hamburg, Germany.*
- Tandon, T. (2016). Women Empowerment: Perspectives and Views, *International Journal of Indian Psychology,* Volume 3, Issue 3, No. 8, DIP: 18.01.134/20160303, ISBN: 978-1-365-12176-0.
- Tzannatos, Z. (1999). Women and Labor Market Changes in the Global Economy: Growth Helps, Inequalities Hurt and Public Policy Matters. *World Development*, *27*(3), 551-569.
- USAID (U.S. Agency for International Development) (2007). Gender-Sensitive Indicators for Economic Growth/Trade-related Activities.
- Wieringa, S. (1998). Rethinking Gender Planning: A Critical Discussion of the Use of the Concept of Gender, Gender, Technology and Development, 2 (3): 349–71.
- Winter, Carolyn. (1994). Working Women in Latin America: Participation, Pay, and Public Policy. *The World Bank LAC Region Technical Department.*

- https://www.oecd.org/employment/50423364.pdf
- https://www.bridge.ids.ac.uk/reports/re40c.pdf
- https://www.iucn.org/sites/dev/files/import/downloads/gender_format.pdf
- http://www.undp.org/content/dam/undp/library/gender/Gender%20and%20 Environment/ Powerful-Synergies.pdf
- https://www.unicef.org/publications/files/pub_humanrights_children_en.pdf
- https://www.worldbank.org/
- https://www.undp.org/content/dam/aplaws/publication/en/publications/ povertyreduction/ poverty-website/taking-action-achieving-gender-equality-and-empoweringwomen/ Taking%20Action-%20Achieving%20Gender%20 Equality%20and%20Empowering%20Women.pdf
- https://www.unfpa.org/resources/issue-7-women-empowerment
- https://sk.sagepub.com/reference/power/n27.xml
- https://en.wikipedia.org/wiki/Steven_Lukes
- https://ophi.org.uk/wp-content/uploads/OPHI-wp04.pdf
- https://documents.worldbank.org/en/publication/documentsreports/ documentdetail/62499 1468764410016/year-in-review
- http://yojana.gov.in/Yojana%20October%20(3).pdf%20-%20final.pdf
- http://www.oecd.org/dev/development-gender/MEASURING-WOMENS-ECONOMICEMPOWERMENT-Gender-Policy-Paper-No-16.pdf
- http://www.oecd.org/gender/Enhancing%20Women%20Economic%20 Empowerment_Fi n_1_Oct_2014.pdf
- https://www.worldbank.org/en/publication/wdr2019
- http://documents1.worldbank.org/curated/en/556251468128407787/pdf/ 359990WDR0co mplete.pdf
- http://documents1.worldbank.org/curated/fr/135051468008418546/pdf/ 343510PAPER0 AF101OFFICIAL0USE0ONLY1.pdf
- http://siteresources.worldbank.org/WBI/Resources/EmpowermentLearning Modulebody. pdf
- Women's Empowerment: What Works? https://doi.org/10.1002/jid.3210
- _________India: Why is women's labour force participation dropping? https:// www.ilo.org/global/about-the-ilo/newsroom/commentanalysis/WCMS_204762/ lang—en/index.html.
- World Bank. 2012. "Indicators: Gender." http://data.worldbank.org/indicator.
- UNESCO. 2003. EFA Global Monitoring Report 2003/4: Gender and Education for All: The Leap to Equality. Paris, France: UNESCO. http:// www.uis.unesco.org/Education/Documents/efa_gmr_2003-4.pdf

Chapter 3

- Budlender, Debbie, Diane Elson, Guy Hewitt and Tanni Mukhopadhyay (2002). Gender Budgets Make Cents: Understanding Gender Responsive Budgets. London: Commonwealth Secretariat.

- Kessler-Harris, A. (2003). *Out to Work: A History of Wage-earning Women in the United States*. Oxford University Press.
- Patel, V. A. (2010). Gender Audit of Budgets in India (2001-2 to 2009-10). *Nivedini*-Journal of Gender Studies, November/December.
- Patel, V. (2014). Gender Responsive Budgets in India. Pragati: Journal of Indian Economy, 1(2), 1-20.
- RUDRA, S. (2018). Gender-Responsive Budgeting, Observer Research Foundation.
- United Nations Economic and Social Commission for Asia and the Pacific (2015). Gender Equality and Women's Empowerment in Asia and the Pacific: Perspectives of Governments on 20 Years of Implementation of the Beijing Declaration and Platform for Action. Bangkok: ESCAP.
- Vibhuti P. (2015). Gender Audit of Budgets in India, Journal of Asian Business Management, Vol. 7, No. 1, January-June.
- https://www.un.org/en/
- https://wcd.nic.in/
- https://www.india.gov.in/
- https://wcd.nic.in/sites/default/files/National%20Policy%20for%20 Empowerment%20of%20Women%202001.pdf
- https://openknowledge.worldbank.org/handle/10986/4391
- http://legislative.gov.in/sites/default/files/A2008-33.pdf
- https://wcd.nic.in/sites/default/files/FinalRFD2013-14_0.pdf
- http://ncw.nic.in/Acts-and-rules/national-commission-women-act-1990-act-no-20-1990- govtof-india
- http://14.139.60.153/bitstream/123456789/2056/1/EIGHTH%20FIVE%20 YEAR%20PLAN%201992-97_D-7346.pdf
- https://niti.gov.in/planningcommission.gov.in/docs/aboutus/committee/strgrp/ stgp_woma n.pdf
- https://mhrd.gov.in/sites/upload_files/mhrd/files/document-reports/ appdraft_1.pdf
- https://www.ediindia.org/
- https://www.epw.in/journal/2016/35/commentary/draft-national-policy-women-2016.html?0=ip_login_no_cache%3D2455afe4ea4499c6dd3380823d38f773
- https://www.researchgate.net/publication/327281499_Sukanya_Samriddhi_ Yojana_India%27s_Innovative_Women_Empowerment_and_Social_Protection_ Scheme
- http://yojana.gov.in/Yojana%20October%20(3).pdf%20-%20final.pdf
- https://tribal.nic.in/
- https://www.ilo.org/wcmsp5/groups/public/ed_emp/emp_policy/documents/ publication/ wcms_234890.pdf
- http://www.nari.nic.in/mahila-shakti-kendra
- https://en.wikipedia.org/wiki/Rajiv_Gandhi_Mahila_Vikas_Pariyojana

Chapter 4

- Agénor, P. R., & Canuto, O. (2015). Gender Equality and Economic Growth in Brazil: a Long-run Analysis. *Journal of Macroeconomics*, *43*, 155-172.
- Cuberes, D., & Teigner, M. (2014). *Agregate Costs of Gender Gaps in the Labor Market: A Quantitative Estimate*. Economic Working Papers, 14 (308): 1-29.
- Daymard, A. (2015). Determinants of Female Entrepreneurship in India, *OECD Economics Department Working Papers, No. 1191,* OECD Publishing, Paris. http://dx.doi.org/10.1787/5js4rfh5gtbq-en
- Duflo, E. (2005). Gender Equality in Development. *BREAD Policy Paper*, *11*(4).
- Duflo, E. (2012). Women Empowerment and Economic Development. *Journal of Economic Literature*, *50*(4), 1051-79.
- Esteve-Volart, B. (2004). Gender Discrimination and Growth: Theory and Evidence from India. http://sticerd.lse.ac.uk/dps/de/dedps42.pdf
- London, T., & Hart, S. L. (2011). Creating a Fortune with the Base of the Pyramid. *Next Generation Business Strategies for the Base of the Pyramid*, 1-18.
- Fujita, M., Krugman, P. R., & Venables, A. (1999). *The Spatial Economy: Cities, Regions, and International Trade*. MIT press.
- Ghani, E., Kerr, W. R., & O'Connell, S. D. (2012). What Makes Cities More Competitive? *Spatial Determinants of Entrepreneurship in India*. The World Bank.
- Klasen, S., & Lamanna, F. (2008). *The Impact of Gender Inequality in Education and* Employment on Economic Growth in Developing Countries: Updates and Extensions (No. 175). Discussion Papers, Ibero America Institute for Economic Research.
- Sorsa, P. (2015). Raising the Economic Participation of Women in India.
- Schumpeter (1936), Opening Doors: The Life and Work of Joseph Schumpeter (Vol. 2). Transaction Publishers.
- Turner, B. S. (Ed.). (1993). Citizenship and Social Theory (Vol. 24). Sage.
- https://www.ilo.org/global/about-the-ilo/newsroom/news/WCMS_324651/lang— en/index.htm
- https://www.worldbank.org/en/research/dime/brief/dime-gender-program
- https://i.dell.com/sites/csdocuments/Corporate_secure_Documents/en/2015-GWELScorecard-Executive-Summary.pdf
- https://www2.deloitte.com/global/en/pages/about-deloitte/articles/global-gender-impactreport. html
- https://www.businesstoday.in/current/economy-politics/women-s-day-2019-femalelabour- force-participation-fall-from-36-in-2005-to-26-in-2018-report/story/325690.html
- https://www.pwc.fr/fr/assets/files/pdf/2019/03/fr-france-pwc-women-in-work-2019.pdf
- https://labour.gov.in/sites/default/files/TheMaternityBenefitAct1961.pd
- https://www.imf.org/external/pubs/ft/sdn/2013/sdn1310.pdf
- https://labour.gov.in/womenlabour/equal-remuneration-acts-and-rules-1976

- https://www.oecd.org/gender/closingthegap.htm
- https://rm.coe.int/16805a1cb6
- https://www.oecd.org/education/school/1855901.pdf.
- dell.com/sites/doccontent/corporate/secure/en/Documents/2015-GWEL-Scorecard-Executive-Summary.pdf

Chapter 5

- Bedford, T. and Burgess, J. (2001). The focus group experience, in: M. LIMB and C. DwYER (Eds) Qualitative Methodologies for Geographers: Issues and Debates, pp. 121-135. Arnold: London.
- Goel, A. (2004). *Education and socio-economic perspectives of women development and empowerment*. Deep and Deep Publications.
- Longhurst, R. (2003). Semi-structured interviews and focus groups. *Key methods in geography*, *3*(2), 143-156.
- McNeill, P., & Chapman, S. (2005). *Research Methods,* Psychology Press.
- Panda, S. M. (2000). Women's Empowerment through NGO Interventions: A Framework for Assessment. *Social Change*, *30*(3-4), 44-63.
- Prince, M., Ferri, C. P., Acosta, D., Albanese, E., Arizaga, R., Dewey, M., & Krishnamoorthy, E. S. (2007). The Protocols for the 10/66 Dementia Research Group Population-based Research Programme. BMC Public Health, 7(1), 165.
- https://www.mavimindia.org/
- https://www.indiastat.com/
- https://wcd.nic.in/
- https://www.pib.gov.in/indexd.aspx

Chapter 6

- Daymard, A. (2015). Determinants of Female Entrepreneurship in India, *OECD Economics Department Working Papers, No. 1191,* OECD Publishing, Paris. http://dx.doi.org/10.1787/5js4rfh5gtbq-en
- De Bruin, A., Brush, C. G., & Welter, F. (2007). Advancing a Framework for Coherent Research on Women's Entrepreneurship. *Entrepreneurship Theory and Practice*, *31*(3), 323-339.
- Duflo, E. (2012). Women Empowerment and Economic Development, *Journal of Economic Literature*, *50*(4), 1051-79.
- Ghani, E., Kerr, W. R., & O'Connell, S. D. (2012). What Makes Cities More Competitive? Spatial Determinants of Entrepreneurship in India. The World Bank.
- Heilbrunn, S. (2004). Impact of Gender on Difficulties Faced by Entrepreneurs. *The International Journal of Entrepreneurship and Innovation*, *5*(3), 159-165.
- Marlow, S. and McAdam, M. (2013). Gender and Entrepreneurship: Advancing Debate and Challenging Myths; Exploring the Mystery of the Underperforming Female Entrepreneur, *International Journal of Entrepreneurial Behavior & Research*, Vol. 19 No. 1, pp. 114-124. https://doi.org/10.1108/13552551311299288.

- Masahisa Fujita, Paul Krugman & Anthony J. Venables (1999). The Spatial Economy, MIT Press Cambridge.
- Sexton, D.L. and Bowman-Upton, N. (1990). Female and Male Entrepreneurs: Psychological Characteristics and Their Role in Gender-Related Discrimination. *Journal of Business Venturing,* 5, 29-36. http://dx.doi.org/10.1016/0883-9026(90)90024 N
- Shah, H. (2013). Creating an Enabling Environment for Women's Entrepreneurship in India. *Development Papers*, *1304*, 15-25.
- Sorsa, P. (2015). Raising the economic participation of women in India, OECD Economics Department Working Papers No. 1185.
- Vecchio, R. P. (2003). Entrepreneurship and Leadership: Common Trends and Common Threads. *Human Resource Management Review*, *13*(2), 303-327.
- http://www.oecd.org/gender/Enhancing%20Women%20Economic%20 Empowerment_Fi n_1_Oct_2014.pdf.
- https://financialservices.gov.in/sites/default/files/F.No_.3452011-AC.pdf.

Chapter 7

- Kalleberg, A. L., & Leicht, K. T. (1991). Gender and Organisational Performance: Determinants of Small Business Survival and Success. Academy of Management Journal, 34(1), 136-161.
- M. Bittman (2001), International Encyclopaedia of the Social & Behavioral Sciences.
- https://www.oakton.edu/user/4/ghamill/Socialist_Feminism.pdf
- https://yourstory.com/mystory/3cfcfd14ef-social-entrepreneurship-is-gainingmomentum- in-india
- https://www.britishcouncil.in/sites/default/files/british_council_se_landscape_in_india_-_report.pdf
- https://www.britishcouncil.org/sites/default/files/social_enterprise_and_womens_empow erment_july.pdf
- http://www.unwomen.org/en/news/in-focus/rural-women-day/2013
- https://www.nabard.org/auth/writereaddata/CareerNotices/1304184040300916363416.pd f
- https://www.nabard.org/
- https://aajeevika.gov.in/
- https://eshakti.nabard.org/
- The state of social enterprise in India https://www.britishcouncil.org/sites/default/files/bc-report-ch4-india-digital_0.pdf
- Social Entrepreneurship in India - https://www.swissnexindia.org/wpcontent/uploads/sites/5/2016/05/Social-Entreprenuership-Report.pdf

Chapter 8

- Daymard, A. (2015). Determinants of Female Entrepreneurship in India, OECD Economics Department Working Papers, No. 1191, OECD Publishing, Paris. http://dx.doi.org/10.1787/5js4rfh5gtbq-en

- Duflo, E. (2012). Women Empowerment and Economic Development. *Journal of Economic Literature*, *50*(4), 1051-79.
- Sorsa, P. (2015). Raising the Economic Participation of Women in India, *OECD Economics Department Working Papers* No. 1185.
- Wittenberg-Cox, A., & Maitland, A. (2008). *Why Women Mean Business: Understanding the Emergence of our Next Economic Revolution*. John Wiley & Sons.
- https://www.oecd.org/newsroom/38528123.pdf
- http://www.oecd.org/greengrowth/40015309.pdf